VALUES AND COMMUNITY IN
MULTI—NATIONAL YUGOSLAVIA

GARY K. BERTSCH

EAST EUROPEAN QUARTERLY, BOULDER
DISTRIBUTED BY COLUMBIA UNIVERSITY PRESS
NEW YORK AND GUILDFORD, SURREY

1976

EAST EUROPEAN MONOGRAPHS, NO. XVII

Gary K. Bertsch is Associate Professor of Political Science
at the University of Georgia.

EAST EUROPEAN MONOGRAPHS

The *East European Monographs* comprise scholarly books on the history and civilization of Eastern Europe. They are published by the *East European Quarterly* in the belief that these studies contribute substantially to the knowledge of the area and serve to stimulate scholarship and research.

1. *Political Ideas and the Enlightenment in the Romanian Principalities, 1750, 1831.* By Vlad Georgescu. 1971.

2. *America, Italy and the Birth of Yugoslavia, 1917-1919.* By Dragan R. Zivojinovic. 1972.

3. *Jewish Nobles and Geniuses in Modern Hungary.* By William O. McCagg, Jr. McCagg, Jr. 1972.

4. *Mixail Soloxov in Yugoslavia: Reception and Literary Impact.* By Robert F. Price. 1973.

5. *The Historical and Nationalistic Thought of Nicolae Iorga.* By William O. Oldson. 1973.

6. *Guide to Polish Libraries and Archives.* By Richard C. Lewanski. 1974.

7. *Vienna Broadcasts to Slovakia, 1938-1939: A Case Study in Subversion.* By Henry Delfiner. 1974.

8. *The 1917 Revolution in Latvia.* By Andrew Ezergailis. 1974.

9. *The Ukraine in the United Nations Organization: A Study in Soviet Foreign Policy, 1944-1950.* By Konstantin Sawczuk. 1975.

10. *The Bosnian Church: A New Interpretation.* By John V. A. Fine, Jr. 1975.

11. *Intellectual and Social Developments in the Hapsburg Empire from Maria Theresa to World War I.* Edited by Stanley B. Winters and Joseph Held. 1975.

12. *Ljudevit Gaj and the Illyrian Movement.* By Elinor Murray Despalatovic. 1975.

13. *Tolerance and Movements of Religious Dissent in Eastern Europe.* Edited by Bela K. Kiraly. 1975.

14. *The Parish Republic: Hlinka's Slovak People's Party, 1939-1945.* By Yeshayahu Jelinek. 1976.

15. *The Russian Annexation of Bessarabia, 1774-1828.* By George F. Jewsbury. 1976.

16. *Modern Hungarian Historiography.* By Steven Bela Vardy. 1976.

17. *Values and Community in Multi-National Yugoslavia.* By Gary K. Bertsch. 1976.

18. *The Greek Socialist Movement and the First World War: The Road to Unity.* By George B. Leon. 1976.

PREFACE

The task of consolidating and governing a multi-national state is not an easy one. Perhaps no party is more sensitive to the difficulties of this task than the post-war Communist leadership in multi-national Yugoslavia. Although Tito and the Partisans' initial success at mobilizing a trans-national resistance movement during World War II was an important beginning, and came to represent the founding of a new Yugoslavia, the post-war building experience has had both its ups and downs. On the positive side, the Yugoslav approach and experience has often been viewed as a model which the fragmented societies of Africa and Asia might emulate. When judging its obvious successes, there appears to be some basis for the growing respect that the Yugoslav approach commands. Compared to earlier fratricidal atrocities characterizing periods both before and during the most recent world war, more recent national relations—which include some level of co-operation and understanding—paint a complimentary picture of the accomplishments of socialist Yugoslavia. Overall, impressive rates of economic growth, innovative advancements in respect to political development, and at least some level of inter-national cooperation seem to lend credence to the value of the Titoist approach.

More recently, however, national-based conflict emanating from some of the republics and provinces once again brought attention to problems within the Yugoslav building experience. During the month of December, 1971, for example, thousands of Croatians in the regional capital of Zagreb participated in a form of political behavior seldom observed in the Communist world. Because of the infrequency of such forms of political activity, the behavior signified an unusual, and one might say, portentous occasion. What was the behavior and what did it represent? Some days before, the Titoist leadership in Belgrade had forced the resignations of high level Croatian leaders, including the First Secretary of the Croatian League of Communists and the President of the Croatian Central Committee. This unsolicited federal intrusion, into what the republic considered its own affairs, provoked mass Croatian demonstrations by supporters of the deposed leaders. Arrests were widespread and security precautions, including the uncommon sight of hovering helicopter patrols, continued until the end of the year. The future of a united Yugoslavia had been threatened, and Tito had moved to eliminate those republic-based leaders failing to protect its unity. Tito accused certain leaders of pandering to nationalists and separatists, and of encouraging anti-socialist factions. As was clear to all observers, and as was clearly displayed by the events of 1971 and 1972, the construction of a genuine community of South Slavic peoples was not yet complete. Uninterrupted communication, cooperation, and understanding—the trademarks of a genuine political community—had yet to come to socialist Yugoslavia.

The post-war building of the Yugoslav socialist community, as represented in the relatively short time frame of twenty-five or thirty years, has been strikingly similar in many ways to the earlier historical experience that stretched over many centuries. While the early South Slavic attempts at a political union, as well as such important commonalities as linguistic and cultural origins, seemed likely to draw the various national groups together, other factors such as national antipathies and foreign rule worked against such consolidation. That is, while the presence of important elements and processes of political integration seemed likely to engender political union, concomitant factors continued to militate against it. In the more recent post-war experience, the same interplay of centrifugal and centripetal forces seem to be at work. While the inter-ethnic attitudes and relations reflected in recent national opinion polls described a more tolerant and cooperative populace better equipped to engender the ideal of "brotherhood and unity," and although certain studies suggested that attitudes would continue to evolve in this more favorable direction, other forces seemed to have had the opposite effect. Specifically, factors and processes seemed to be at work which tended to exacerbate rather than attenuate national based conflict.

Although the overall process of community-building is a complex one, and likely to be comprised of a variety of inter-related components, one of the central components seems to be of human nature. This dimension of community-building represents the attitudes and values held by the populace, and concerns the relationship that such belief systems have upon the growth or decline of a genuine socialist community. It is this question that will draw the attention of this book. In the pages to follow, we will attempt to describe the Yugoslav populace by examining their attitudes and values. We will focus upon those values purported to be closely related to the idea of community-building, and attempt to determine how these values are changing, and are likely to change in future years. Finally, related forces appearing to affect the human dimension of community-building will be examined. We will atttempt to determine, for example, what forces were at work and appear to have caused the "nationalist revival" permeating Yugoslavia in the early 1970's. These and related questions are the fundamental issues to be pursued in this book.

Finally, it should be noted that two major concerns motivated this study. The first involves the belief that the evolution of the Yugoslav socialist community, particularly in terms of individual values and behavior, is an important subject well worth investigating. The search of smaller nations for a satisfactory and profitable place in a larger political federation reveals an interesting chronicle and an important issue for political research. The manner in which different individuals and groups in Yugoslavia view and affect this search is a story that this study will attempt to record.

The second concern involves what the Yugoslav experience might reveal in respect to larger, worldwide patterns. Motivated by the goals of comparative social science research, this study will attempt to approach the subject of community-building in a way that will facilitate comparison with other societies and other cultures. This comparativist perspective is based upon the value that the processes of community-building in multinational Yugoslavia will be best understood when comparing them with the patterns found in other societies. Even though this study is already cross-national in the sense that it compares relationships across the various nations of Yugoslavia, it is further hoped that it will offer an approach and methodology that can be expanded to other political and cultural settings.

The author embarked on the study hoping to do justice to the complexity of the Yugoslav building process—and to the Yugoslavs' own view of this phenomenon—as well as to the methodology of contemporary social science. Admittedly, the present state of social science research is likely to do certain injustices to the infinite complexities of socio-political phenomena such as that represented by the question of community-building. At the same time, the question is an unusually sensitive one that has too often been approached on the basis of an author's personal biases, or from the perspective of his own nation's national self-interests. The consequence has often been less than objective treatments of the question. The question is much too important for this sort of consideration and deserves a fairer treatment. While the author makes no pretensions about total objectivity, he has taken great pains to approach the subject in a way that is guided and disciplined by scientific data. Moreover, since the author has no ties to any of the Yugoslav nations or ethnic groups—although in the course of years he has developed a deep affection for all of them—he has not felt an obligation to show special preference to any. It goes without saying that the author felt that a study which approached the sensitive question of Yugoslav community-building disciplined by the methods of modern social science could aid in an overall understanding of the subject.

The author remembers with special gratitude the guidance and assistance provided by Professor M. George Zaninovich of the University of Oregon. It was under Professor Zaninovich's instruction that the author initially became interested and involved in the research surrounding this work. Professor Zaninovich not only kindled the author's interest in Yugoslavia, but also was responsible for the original research project that provides a good part of the data base for this study.

The author is indebted to a number of institutions for providing support that enabled the study and writing of this book. First, the Project on the Comparative Study of Communist Societies, University of California, provided financial support for the survey work carried out by the Center for Public Opinion Research of the Institute of Social Sciences, Belgrade, Yugoslavia. Secondly, the Institute for International Studies and Overseas Administration of the University of Oregon provided a summer research fellowship, and the International Research and Exchanges Board provided a generous exchange fellowship that allowed the author's research and study in Yugoslavia. Finally, the University of Georgia and the Institute on East Central Europe, Columbia University, provided the author with generous research time which aided the completion of this study.

It is not possible in this short space to acknowledge the assistance of all the persons who contributed in some way to the overall study. Many Yugoslavs and Americans alike made a variety of generous contributions. For this support and counsel the author is sincerely grateful. The author also would like to acknowledge a very special debt to his wife Joan, who not only typed untold numbers of rough drafts of the manuscript and contributed at all phases of the research, but also managed to bring both pleasure and profit to all of our research expeditions.

TABLE OF CONTENTS

Page

PREFACE v

LIST OF TABLES xii

LIST OF FIGURES xiv

CHAPTER

1. THE QUESTION OF COMMUNITY-BUILDING 3
   A. Introduction
   B. Historical Developments

2. COMMUNITY-BUILDING AND SOCIAL CHANGE. . 9
   A. Introduction
   B. Approaching the Subject of
      Community-Building
   C. Importance of Community-
      Building in the Yugoslav
      Setting
   D. The Theoretical Bases: Back-
      ground of the Problem
   E. The Human Differences

3. CONCEPTUALIZING THE RELATIONSHIP
   BETWEEN INDIVIDUAL CHANGE AND
   COMMUNITY-BUILDING. 37
   A. Introduction
   B. Methodology
   C. Conceptual Framework
   D. Ordering the Variables

4. SOCIAL MOBILIZATION AND CHANGING
   VALUE SYSTEMS: COUNTRY-WIDE OB-
   SERVATIONS 52
   A. Introduction
   B. Characteristics of Mobilization
   C. Value Characteristics
   D. Application of the Model

Page

CHAPTER

5. MOBILIZATION AND VALUE CHANGE:
   THE EFFECT OF NATIONALITY AND
   DEVELOPMENTAL VARIABLES 75
   A. Introduction
   B. Controlling for Country-Wide
      Diversity
   C. Potential Intervening Influences
   D. Cross-National Comparisons: The
      Slovene, Croat, Serb, and Mace-
      donian Samples
   E. Communal Comparisons: Controlling
      for Level of Socio-Economic
      Development

6. PATTERNS OF MOBILIZATION AND
   CHANGE TENDENCY 93
   A. Introduction
   B. Mobilization and Attitude Change:
      Applying the Controls

7. UNIVERSALISTIC ATTTUDES AND A
   REVIVAL OF NATIONALISM 106
   A. Introduction
   B. Additional Attitude Surveys
   C. Contemporary Nationalisms:
      Problems, Fears, and
      Frustrations
   D. Relative Deprivation: The Root of
      Frustrations and Nationalisms
   E. Relative Deprivation and Separatism:
      The Croatian Example
   F. Relative Deprivation and Unitarism:
      The Serbian Example
   G. Possible Alternatives

8. THE INDIVIDUAL IN YUGOSLAVIA:
   IMPLICATIONS RAISED FOR AN
   EVOLVING SOCIALIST COMMUNITY 124
   A. Introduction
   B. The Yugoslav Pattern

Page

APPENDICES. 133

NOTES 137

LIST OF TABLES

Table   Page

1. Radio, Television, and Newspaper
   Utilization by Exposure Level 54

2. Importance of the Role of Supernatural
   Forces by Education 56

3. Importance of the Role of Supernatural
   Forces by Mass Media Exposure 58

4. Importance of the Role of Supernatural
   Forces by Internal Travel 58

5. Importance of the Role of Supernatural
   Forces by External Travel 59

6. Importance of Parental Authority
   by Education 60

7. Importance of Parental Authority
   by Mass Media Exposure 61

8. Importance of Parental Authority
   by Internal Travel 61

9. Correlation Matrix: Items Comprising
   Social Mobilization Index and
   Modernism Scale 64

10. Correlation Matrix: Items Comprising
    Social Mobilization Index and
    Cultural Universalism Scale 65

11. Correlation Matrix: Items Comprising
    Modernism Scale and
    Cultural Universalism Scale 66

12. Importance of One's Own Dialect
    by Importance of Parental Authority 67

13. Willingness to Communicate
    by Belief in Supernatural Forces. 68

14. Level of Modernism
    by Level of Mobilization. 71

15. Level of Cultural Universalism
    by Level of Modernism. 71

Table   Page

16. Distribution of Instruments of Mass Media
    by Republic 78

17. Age of Respondent
    by Level of Mobilization 94

18. Social and Political Status
    by Level of Mobilization 95

19. Membership in the League of Communists
    by Level of Mobilization 97

20. Coefficients Summarizing Relationships
    for Three Age Groups 99

21. Coefficients Summarizing Relationships
    for Three Socio-Political Status Groups 101

22. Coefficients Summarizing Relationships
    for Communist Party
    Membership Groups 103

23. Inter-Ethnic Relations in Yugoslavia, 1964 107

24. Ethnic Distance in Yugoslavia, 1966 108

LIST OF FIGURES

Figure   Page

1. Variables in the Change Model 24

2. Arrow Diagram Representing the
     Conceptualization of Individual Change. 45

3. Continuum Based Upon the Three Criteria
     Assessing the Relative Extent of
     Community Development. 47

4. Conceptualization of A_1, B_2, and C_3 with
     Nationality Controlled 50

5. Three Variable Model with Suggested
     Strengths of Relationship 65

6. Three Variable Model:
     Country-Wide Sample. 70

7. Three Variable Model with
     Mobilization Controlled 72

8. Three Variable Model with
     Modernism Controlled 73

9. Three Variable Model: Slovenes 82

10. Three Variable Model: Croats. 84

11. Three Variable Model: Serbs. 85

12. Three Variable Model: Macedonians. 86

13. Three Variable Model: Individuals Inhabiting
      Most Developed Communes. 89

14. Three Variable Model: Individuals Inhabiting
      Developed Communes 89

15. Three Variable Model: Individuals Inhabiting
      Less Developed Communes 90

16. Three Variable Model: Individuals Inhabiting
      Least Developed Communes 91

17. Relative Deprivation: Croats. 115

18. Relative Deprivation: Serbs 120

THE GREEK SOCIALIST MOVEMENT
AND THE FIRST WORLD WAR:
THE ROAD TO UNITY

CHAPTER I

THE QUESTION OF COMMUNITY-BUILDING

I. Introduction

The questions of cultural particularism and nationalism continue to pose serious challenges to leaders of multi-national states who hope to mold political community in settings of ethno-cultural diversity.[1] Events resulting from the multi-national condition in Yugoslavia suggest that this socialist state possesses no special immunity from this larger, world-wide pattern. For although the development of a Yugoslav socialist community (*Jugoslovenska socijalistička zajednica*) has been a foremost goal of the Titoist regime, the recurrence of national-based conflict indicates persisting difficulties in the achievement of this ideal.[2]

The task of community-building in a diverse multi-national society is not an easy one, and to criticize the Titoist strategy, or to underemphasize or discredit the Yugoslav's progress, would be patently unfair. Moreover, one might reasonably argue that the Yugoslav achievements have been remarkable, particularly in view of the historical difficulties of pre-War Yugoslavia. None of the atrocities committed before or during World War II, for example, have been repeated in the Titoist state. Furthermore, the ethnic, religious, or racial violence evidenced in a number of so-called developed states (e.g., Canada, Great Britain and the United States), not to mention such less developed examples as Nigeria or Sudan, has been far more serious than in multi-national Yugoslavia. At the same time, however, the fact remains that manifestations of nationalism and particularism are still being expressed in Yugoslavia over a quarter of a century after the establishment of a Marxist system that so fervidly sought to resolve the historical animosities by replacing them with "brotherhood and unity."[3]

II. Historical Developments

Although the establishment of a political union of South Slavic nationalities is of recent origin, the concept goes back for centuries in history.

Various "Pan-Slavic" movements arose before the twentieth century (e.g., the nineteenth century Illyrian movement), although none was successful in uniting the diverse South Slavic groups into a common political state. It was not until the end of the First World War, in fact, that the "ideal"— unification—was given practical political expression. Shortly after the 1918 "union" of the Kingdom of Serbs, Croats, and Slovenes, however, the traditional jealousies and inevitable difficulties of political union brought historical animosities to the surface.[4] King Alexander, the Serbian monarch entrusted with the difficult task of creating and integrating a modern nation-state from the rubble of centuries of imperial administration and subsequent war devastation, made little if any progress toward the ideal. In fact, most would contend that the interwar Royalist dictatorship succeeded only in exacerbating existing national tensions, and ultimately, willed a fragmented and ungovernable populace to the hands of the Fascist invaders.

In the subsequent political vacuum existing at the time of the Nazi invasion, little semblance of unity or cooperation existed. But although the population and resistance movements split into a variety of national-based factions (e.g., the pro-Serbian Chetniks led by Mihailović, and the Nazi oriented Ustashi led by the Croat Pavelić), some sentiment still remained in support of a broader Yugoslav idea. The pro-Yugoslav and anti-Fascist socialist sentiment was seized and built upon by Tito and his Partisans, who successfully enlisted resistance forces from across the various nationalities and ethnic groups. Through the ensuing wartime struggle and the successful Partisan resistance movement, the victorious Communists established a broad basis for cross-national cooperation. But the presence of wartime cooperation did not mean that the Partisans were to return from battle with a fully unified society. For although the transnational Partisan movement gained some measure of unity against the threat of the invading Nazis, it subsequently could not fully assuage the bitter memories which persisted at the end of the war. Although the Croat Tito, for example, was likely to guard against the (re)establishment of a Greater Serbian state, Croatian fears of Serbian domination remained. In addition, most of the other nationalties and ethnic minorities nursed national-based grievances of one sort or another.

In order to deal with the multi-national condition and all of the attendant difficulties in those early years of development, the post-war Communist regime emulated the federal structure of the Soviet state. Under the federal system, each of the major Slavic groups (Slovenes, Croats, Serbs, Montenegrins, and Macedonians) was granted a republic within which its language and culture would predominate. An additional republic, Bosnia-Hercegovina, was established to include the diverse Serb,

Croat, and Slavic Moslem (or Bosniak) inhabitants of this mountainous heartland region. Finally, two autonomous provinces were established for the two largest non-Slavic minorities, the Hungarians in Vojvodina and the Albanians in Kosovo. This regional structure, representing the federal political formula of the new state, was set out in Article 1 of the original Constitution:

> The Federative People's Republic of Yugoslavia is a federal people's state, republican in form, a community of peoples equal in rights, who, on the basis of the right of self-determination, including the right of separation, have expressed their will to live together in a federative state.

The phrase in this article, "a community of peoples," represents the special problem confronting the Yugoslav leaders—namely, how to build an integrated community from a mosaic of diverse and often conflicting peoples. The difficulties result from the heterogeneous mixture of South Slavic peoples, all of which possess distinct cultural traditions and separate national identities. At the same time, the prospect of a wider community of peoples, based upon equal rights and including—at least theoretically— the ultimate right of separation, represented the hope and idea for a united South Slavic state.

The new regime's initial community-building strategy was that based upon the idea of "Yugoslavism," a policy tending toward political and economic centralization.[5] During this temporary stage, which is referred to by Yugoslavs as the administrative phase of development, manifestations of nationalism tended to be repressed in the quest for a unified society. Under this approach, the party leadership envisioned the rapid development of a higher order, South Slavic identity and a sense of Yugoslav nationhood. The underlying rationale for this strategy was that a new, supra-national identity would evolve along with the dissolution of more traditional (e.g., national, religious, and cultural) attachments.

Through the fifties and early sixties, the Yugoslav leaders attempted to strike a delicate balance between unity and diversity, or centralism versus federalism. While working toward the ideal of unity, they were cautious not to exhibit undue disrespect for the national units from which the multi-national state was comprised. But due to the necessities of post-war development, and a variety of external events of major import (e.g., the Trieste question, the Cominform expulsion), the Titoist building strategy was inclined toward centralism.

By the middle of the 1960's, however, the idea of Yugoslavism, and the more centralistic policy it implied, was almost entirely discredited. It became increasingly apparent to the leadership that the former attachments to national cultures, traditions, and interests were not to be easily dissolved into the more abstract notion of a higher order Yugoslav identity. To some national groups, the centralist policy smacked of assimilation and represented an overt threat to their own identities and cultures. In addition, most of the non-Serb groups tended to associate the more centralistic strategy with the idea of a "Greater Serbia." Hence, the policy of Yugoslavism was perceived by most groups as threatening and, therefore, seemed to intensify rather than dissolve national differences.

During the period of 1946-65, then, a variety of forces were working against the centralist strategy. Perhaps the most significant was the reform policy of political and economic decentralization which allocated increasing power to the republics and lower level political units. As one might surmise, the centralism emphasized under the older policy, and the decentralization of the new reforms, represented a contradiction so that by the early 1960's, the former policy and any mention of Yugoslavism began to fade. In contrast to the earlier policy, which tended toward a centralist approach, the new phase seemed to be guided by the "four D's": decentralization, deetatization, depoliticalization, and democratization. The resultant policy placed greater importance on national (i.e., regional) autonomy and the decentralization of decision-making power. The reform movement picked up steam through the late 1960's and culminated in the far-reaching set of constitutional amendments approved by the Federal Assembly on June 30, 1971.[6] According to many observers, the constitutional changes made the republics the key units of government and took the Yugoslavs near to a confederation type system.

Although subsequent developments made both implementation and interpretation of the amendments somewhat problematical, the major purpose of this set of constitutional changes was to further delimit the functions and responsibilities of the central government, while simultaneously expanding them on the regional and local level. The general uncertainty and debate surrounding the amendments was high, however, and further heightened by what Tito and the "hardliners" perceived in late 1971 as "nationalist deviations" within certain sectors of the populace, and more significantly, within high organs of the League of Communists of Yugoslavia (LCY). Tito's initial response to the "national excesses" was the forced resignation and replacement of the highest level Croatian leaders (including Secretary of the Croatian League of Communists, Miko Tripalo, and President of the Croatian Central Committee, Savka Dabčević-Kučar) in December of 1971.

What was initially viewed in some quarters as an anti-Croat campaign soon developed into a country-wide reorganization of the republic level leadership. During 1972, the LCY leadership structure underwent a major reshuffling throughout the country, and led to the forced resignations of such respected leaders as Marko Nikezić and Latinka Perović, President and Secretary of the Serbian Central Committee, respectively. For the first time since the war, party leaders (including Tito) began to speak of a national crisis which was threatening the unity of socialist Yugoslavia. The initial LCY response to the national situation blossomed into a broader political movement which severely attacked the "enemies" of Yugoslav socialism, including "etatistic bureaucratism, technocratism, nationalism, and all anti-self-managing and anti-socialist tendencies."[7] The main feature of this movement was the assault by Tito and the "hardliners" (notably Stane Dolanc, Jure Bilić, and others) on what they considered to be the revival of nationalism in some sectors of the society, including high-level LCY officials within some of the constituent republics.

The serious concern accorded the national situation was evidenced by the attention given it in 1972 by the Yugoslav Party Presidium. At the Thirty-Fourth Session of the Presidium held July 11 and 12 on the island of Brioni, for example, five members of the Presidium (Todo Kurtović, Edvard Kardelj, Latinka Perović, Milka Planinc, and Veljko Vlahović) lashed out at nationalistic tendencies of two major forms. Their identification of the forms was noteworthy in the sense that it criticized not only the idea of "separatism," but also the notion of "unitarism." This latter form of nationalism had not been subjected to open criticism in the past although it had always been associated more closely with the Serbs and the policy of Yugoslavism. The "separatist" variety, on the other hand, had been more closely associated with Croatian nationalism and viewed a brighter future for Croatia outside of the Yugoslav federation. The more recent criticism of the "unitarist" variety and the lumping of the two varieties was intended to counter feelings that the central party leadership was carrying on an anti-Croat campaign. Overall, the party's strategy was to break the power of the strong regional party organization in the interest of greater unity and recentralization with the LCY structure. In the view of the central leadership, the excesses of decentralization and the concomitant revival of nationalism required a reassertion of anti-nationalist and pro-Yugoslav forces. Such forces were to be found in the revitalized ranks of the LCY.

These movments toward ideological centralization within the context of a decentralized federal state system culminated with two important events in 1974. The first, the adoption of a new Constitution in the early spring of that year, formalized the political structure within which the state was to operate. The second, the Tenth Party Congress held in May of that year, emphasized and attempted to legitimate the leading role of the LCY in this operation. Although of a broader significance, both events were very much influenced by and tied to the persistent problem of national relations within the multi-national state.

In summary, then, it is not unfair to say that various forms of nationalism continue to be major and irritating political forces within the Yugoslav system.[8] To the credit of the LCY leadership, it should be noted that they have been willing to acknowledge that these difficulties exist (unlike the leadership in some other socialist states) and are unwilling to view them as simply characteristics or a residue of the capitalist system. The important question of concern to this analysis, however, asks why such manifestations of nationalism and particularism still exist in a Marxist society which had worked so fervidly for their demise. Do manifestations exist because the populace has been unwilling or unable to bury the animosities and differences of the past? Furthermore, has there been any attitude change concerning these issues within the Yugoslav populace over the post-war years, and if so, what has been the nature of the change? Also, what factors seem to be at work in the Yugoslav environment that tend to bring about attitude change? And finally, how do these and other factors relate to national identity and to the broader community-building process within the Yugoslav federation? These and other related questions represent the underlying themes of this book.

CHAPTER II

COMMUNITY BUILDING AND SOCIAL CHANGE

A. *Introduction*

This is a study of community-building in Yugoslavia and some phenomena that affect it. As noted above, the early historical development of the South Slavs, as well as more recent events and circumstances, have raised certain questions about the possibilities for the establishment and growth of a sense of political community in the modern Yugoslav setting. This study will seek to show that although the natural forces of social and economic development characterizing the post-war system are effecting the building process, they still must be viewed in conjunction with other important environmental and historical forces.

It is commonly held that economic development affects social and political evolution. This belief envisions a relationship between industrialization and society, and further, between industrialization and the individual. At the same time, rather limited empirical knowledge has been offered concerning the connection between economic and social change, and changes in individual characteristics and value systems.

The study at hand focuses on this relationship within the developing Yugoslav system. The economic changes over the post-war years in Yugoslavia have represented a definite trend toward greater industrialization, which in turn, has clearly affected changes in some social aspects of the system. A number of these social phenomena will be of concern here—namely, increased education, exposure to the mass media, and the cultural contact brought about by increasing travel rates. This investigation will consider the influence of such social changes upon the belief systems of individuals.[1] It is to be contended that these social changes, as well as the values they affect, have potential importance to the further evolution of community within Yugoslav society.

Interest is taken in belief systems because of the relationship between the value orientations of individuals comprising a political system and certain attributes of that system. The basis for suggesting such a relationship results from the findings of empirical studies carried out by other scholars. The work of Almond and Verba in *The Civic Culture* suggests, for example, "that in the more stable democracies there does exist a particular set of political attitudes that could theoretically further the chances of stable democracy."[2] This study maintains in a similar fashion that a particular set of individual characteristics and values *may* engender the stable, and yet dynamic, construction of a new and modern South Slavic community.

The focus, therefore, is upon the individual within a setting that has undergone massive and far-reaching changes in all spheres of its economic, political, and social environment. Within this kind of changing environment, the individual is an interesting and rather crucial focus of analysis. There is much that is unknown about the individual Yugoslav and his relationship to the changes taking place around him. For example, has the individual inhabiting the system changed, and if so, in what manner? Stated simply, it seems important to have a better idea of man's relationship to his environment. In order to accomplish this, it is necessary to determine the manner of individual change, the nature of the influencing phenomena, and the dynamics of the change process.

After viewing social and economic statistics over the post-war years, it can not be disputed that the setting surrounding the individual in Yugoslav society is changing at a very rapid rate. This study will suggest that the alteration of surroundings is also having a definite, traceable effect upon the individual. One only needs to look as far as any major city in present-day Yugoslavia to view some of the ramifications of this phenomenon. One of the most apparent is the manner of dress. In this respect, the differences are readily apparent between those who have been separated from the influences of their changing environment (e.g., those in isolated villages) and those who have not. Those who read the newspapers, the fashion magazines, and travel to Italy, Austria, and elsewhere are likely to dress in a rather different manner than those unable or unwilling to read or travel. In other words, some individuals are "touched" by changes in their environment while others are not. Those who are suggest the presence of a new sector in contemporary Yugoslavia. This sector represents individuals who are exposed to and affected by the environmental changes of a modernizing society.

The notion of the foregoing differences suggests that the social and economic changes characterizing a developing country may not be distributed evenly throughout the system. The changes experienced by the villager are quite likely to be different from those reaching the urbane city dweller. Consequently, while there is reason to speak of an overall process of individual change, it should not be forgotten that certain groups or individuals may be affected differently. First of all, some groups may be characterized by different "starting-points." For example, because of their traditional physical isolation from the outside world, villagers are likely to have begun with rather different belief systems than individuals tied more closely to the urban centers. Furthermore, some groups may be exposed to different influencing stimuli. These impinging stimuli may differ not only in kind but also in degree. Therefore, research on the rate and scope of individual change must take into account the fact that different persons may be affected in contrasting manners because of variations in both group characteristics and the nature of the impinging change stimuli. Therefore, the problem at hand has many requirements. First, it necessitates a definite conceptualization of the process of indvidual change, as well as a firm understanding of the influences that encourage or facilitate the process. Then, it requires some comprehension of the relationship between individual change and the community-building process. Finally, it necessitates some empirical method to identify the rate and scope of individual change within the Yugoslav populace.

Modern methods in the social sciences allow us to approach these requirements with some measure of success. However, a survey of the literature shows no great effort to undertake this study of the individual as it relates to the process of community-building in non-American contexts. On the one hand, the individual has been examined so exhaustively in the field of American electoral studies, that the discipline has become saturated with articles, monographs, and reference-type volumes on social and political behavior. On the other hand, however, the individual in non-American contexts and in different situations has not received a commensurate amount of attention. Daniel Lerner's landmark study of modernization in the Middle East, Harvard's study by the Center for International Affairs of the causes and consequences of individual changes in six developing countries, and the Almond and Verba study of democracy in five nations are significant attempts to rectify this lack of research in the general area of individual and social change.[3] However, it must be admitted that while both individuals and societies are undergoing rapid and incalculable change, we still know very little about the dynamics and stimuli that affect this process.

There comes a time in the development of any field of study when one becomes discontent with the usual pessimism discouraging this sort of work, such as the often heard contention that "social phenomena are too complex to permit systematic analysis of causal factors." While neither overlooking the controversies surrounding the word "cause" in the social sciences nor discounting the complexity of social phenomena, this study will approach the subject in terms of causal analysis. A definite, planned strategy has been developed to permit this type of approach. It involves both a systematic conceptualization of Yugoslav development as well as some important statistical assumptions.

First, the process of economic development in Yugoslavia was carefully reviewed through longitudinal analysis of statistical sources. This developmental process was determined to be associated with certain social changes within the system.[4] Then, through the use of survey data the study viewed individuals who were coming into contact with some of these social changes.[5] Through cross-sectional analysis, individuals who had been exposed to more extensive social change were compared to those exposed to lower levels. In other words, highly educated, exposed, and traveled individuals were compared to those with an absence of such characteristics. This cross-sectional analysis identified differences in value systems and suggested a causal influence resulting from these social changes. In effect, after operationalizing the relevant individual variables and making the necessary statistical assumptions, it was possible to identify a longitudinal causal pattern through cross-sectional analysis.[6]

Therefore, while reviewing the process of economic development, some concomitant factors of social change were identified through survey analysis of a sample of over 1100 Yugoslavs. These factors, which appeared to alter individual value systems, were used to construct an index called social mobilization. This index was then placed into a chain of variables operationalized at the individual level of analysis. After ordering this chain according to a number of statistical assumptions and the time sequence involved, it was found that this index of social factors encouraged a certain configuration of values that appeared to be closely tied to the community-building process in Yugoslavia. The identified pattern may not only help explain some dynamics of the community-building process today, but may also offer predictions for the future due to the projected proliferation of mobilization stimuli in the coming years.

When approaching the infinitely complex subject of Yugoslav development, one is faced with choosing between a "macro" and "micro" approach to the subject.[7] By focusing specifically on social mobilization and changing value patterns, this study has obviously opted for the "micro" alternative. This narrow concern with value change among the citizenry has made the author feel on more than one occasion that he was missing perhaps the most important ingredients in the change process—namely, the values and actions of higher-level political and economic elites within the country. However, one remark in a most interesting and important book by Paul Shoup on Yugoslav development addressed itself to this point in the following fashion:

> Changes in national attitudes are difficult to measure, and cannot
> be gauged simply in terms of the intensity of the political or
> economic disputes carried on by a small percentage of the popu-
> lation. This was true in the interwar period, and remains the case
> today.[8]

Shoup is of course correct. It is easy to disregard or perhaps unintentionally overlook the values of the country-wide populace while listening to the "clamor" of the minority who reach the newspapers and television screens. While not overlooking the central role and opinions of elites,* the author will contend that over the long run, the values of the masses are an extremely important and perhaps the most crucial ingredient in the community-building process and, in the final analysis, will determine whether a complex and diverse set of peoples such as the Yugoslavs can live cooperatively and profitably within the structure of a modern and unified federal political system. The design of this study, therefore, aspires to shed light on the nature of country-wide systems in Yugoslavia with a hope of providing a better understanding of the present and a basis for predicting future changes.

B. Approaching the Subject of Community-Building and the Individual

To gain some understanding of the community-building process in Yugoslavia requires the selection of a working vocabulary that accurately describes the relevant phenomena. The selected vocabulary must fulfill a number of conditions. First, the concepts must identify the most important phenomena in the change process. Second, the terms must be operational and conducive to testing and measurement. And third, the vocabulary used in this study must accurately describe the subject matter for foreign, Yugoslav, and American readers.

Before looking for such a vocabulary, it might be important to briefly sketch the process of community-building and some of the major issues and concepts of relevance to it. In that regard, it will be briefly noted that the peoples of Yugoslavia are being reached by a new type of environmental change brought about by the Communist revolution and the ensuing years of rapid economic and social development. As a result, it is reasonable to argue that the process of individual modernization is reaching and changing the value systems of large sectors of the population. One important question arising during this process of individual modernization relates to any possible accompanying change in regard to the objects commanding an individual's allegiance or identification. Namely, in Yugoslavia the modernizing citizenry is placed between two interdependent but—due to requirements of community-building—potentially conflicting attachments. One represents the more particularistic identification associated with family, locale, language, norms, and nationality, while the second pertains to the more impersonal identity associated with a larger, modern socialist community. The former set of attachments reflects a more personal, provincial orientation and the latter reflects a universal identity

*Chapter VII is devoted to this topic.

associated with a modern socialist community envisioned by the post-war Communist leadership.

Since the idea of community as used in this study is based upon communication, cooperation, and understanding, it should be noted that the former set of particularistic orientations can and have represented potential barriers to community development in Yugoslav society. Social relations based upon familial ties, localism, and national and linguistic differences have been in the past and are still in the present impediments to the development of a genuine sense of political community in the Yugoslav state. However, with the further evolution of the socialist state and possibility for changing value systems, it may be found that social relations of a new kind will become more important and perhaps eventually replace the older relations based upon more provincial attachments. Marx himself expressed the philosophy in somewhat less uncertain terms when he noted that within the socialist state the class struggle would inevitably diminish national and other more provincial loyalties. If attachments to these former loyalties could be dissolved in fact, it might be found that individuals could relate to each other more as members of a common political community and less as members of some particular social grouping (e.g., national, religious, or lingual). This change in value systems in turn may engender the communication, cooperation and understanding needed to develop and bind a diverse society such as the Yugoslav.

This briefly sketched set of phenomena and the process they represent will be called community-building. The first part of the ensuing section will discuss the reasons for using the term community-building to represent the process, while the second will move on to the particular, individual phenomena that characterize the process.

Definitional Considerations

A number of definitional problems arise when approaching the idea of community-building and individual change in the modern nation-state. The problem of terminology is even more complicated in the case of Yugoslavia where the Serbo-Croatian terms *zajednica* (community), *narod* (people or nation), and *narodnost* (nationality) take on a particular complexity because of the special, multinational characteristics of the land. This complexity is complicated further by the increasing use of two international terms within the country, *nacija* (nation) and *nacionalnost* (nationality). Although these two terms possess some special connotations and uses in the Yugoslav context, and are more widely used among the higher educated or the "international" segments of the society, they are increasingly being used as synonyms for *narod* and *narodnost*.[9]

The immediate problem confronting the study was whether to call the process "nation-building" as has been largely done by other scholars interested in the subject, or to select a new term such as "community-building" which might be more applicable in the Yugoslav context.[10] The study chose the latter alternative for three primary reasons.

The first reason for avoiding the use of the term nation to describe the development process results from the simple fact that Yugoslavia is composed of a number of nations. Irrespective of whose conception of the term is considered, the multi-national composition of the country remains unchangeable. The definitions of nation offered by both Marxist and non-Marxist writers lead to the same conclusion: that Yugoslavia is and should be viewed as a socialist community formed from a number of smaller nations.

According to perhaps the most often cited Marxist theoretician on the nationality issue, Joseph V. Stalin, a nation is based upon five characteristic features. He writes: "A nation is a historically evolved stable community of language, territory, economic life, and psychological make-up manifested in a community of culture."[11] According to Stalin's definition, the historical features and special circumstances of Yugoslav development have been such to create a number of nations within the modern Yugoslav state. Slovenia, Croatia, Serbia, Macedonia, Montenegro, and possibly others can be and have been called nations on the basis of Stalin's five criteria.[12] Therefore, in terms of Stalin's conception, it is clear that Yugoslavia can more accurately be called a community or federation of nations, than it can a single South Slavic nation.[13]

The leading Yugoslav theoretician on the nationality issue, Edvard Kardelj, adds another condition essential to the definition of a nation. Namely, he considers the factors that Stalin listed as essential and also adds one of his own, "the social division of labor in the epoch of capitalism." Kardelj's definition of a nation takes the following form:

> A specific community of peoples arising on the basis of the social
> division of labor in the epoch of capitalism, in a compact territory
> and within the framework of a common language and close ethnic
> and cultural similarity in general.[14]

Although the definition would seem to be interpreted as an acknowledgement and defense of the separate nations in Yugoslavia due to its inclusion of the "common language and close ethnic and cultural similarity" phrase, one scholar of the Yugoslav national question argues that it was designed for another purpose.[15] That is, it appears that Kardelj's definition and his larger analysis was intended to defend each nation-state's right within the Communist movement, rather than the existence of the separate South Slavic nations. However, there is some inconsistency and vagueness evidenced if Kardelj argues for the integrity and rights of socialist nations, and then implies that it does not fully apply to those nations within Yugoslavia.[16] It is clear, however, that just as in Stalin's conception, Kardelj's words can be interpreted to support the multi-national character of Yugoslavia.

The second reason for selecting a term other than nation to describe the building process results from the complexity and unavoidable confusion that the term raises in the Yugoslav context. According to the widely accepted definitions of nation and other closely associated terms, Yugoslavia represents a complex configuration of peoples, nations, and nationalities that are difficult to sort out and classify in any systematic manner. After reviewing the conceptions of the most noted writers on the phenomena, the following definitions could be offered.[17] *People* is a term referring to any group of individuals who have a certain characteristic or number of characteristics in common. For example, the inhabitants of the northernmost section of the country, the Slovenes, may be referred to as a people because of their common language (Slovenian), their territory, religion (Catholicism), traditions, and other common characteristics. A *nationality*, in turn, is a people such as the Slovenes who enjoy a significant amount of political, economic, social, and cultural organization and autonomy. That is to say that among this grouping of people who call themselves Slovenes, there is a considerable amount of interchange and activity in political, economic, social, and cultural affairs; furthermore, this interchange is carried on in the language and style of the people. *Nation*, then, can be used to refer to people such as the Slovenes who are living in a political unit of their own and who are enjoying this organization and autonomy of activity. The difference between a people and a nation is that in the first, a commonality among the people may exist but there may be little effort or opportunity to practice, make use of, or enjoy this commonality. However, in a nation there is a definite level of activity based upon such a common set of attributes.

According to these three basic definitions, one might speak of five or more processes of nation-building within Yugoslavia.[18] That is, if Slovenia can be viewed as a nation according to the traditional conceptions, and therefore recognized as involved in a process of nation-building, all other national units in the Yugoslav state can also be viewed in a similar process of national development.[19] What is being suggested is that these conceptions of the three terms are confronted by a great deal of confusion and many difficulties in the Yugoslav context. For example, while one might feel comfortable in calling Slovenia a people as well as a nation, can the inhabitants of Bosnia-Hercegovina be referred to in the same manner?[20] Furthermore, what happens in the situation of Kosovo, where over two-thirds of the people are Albanian, of Moslem religious confession, and of similar cultural traits and traditions?

Official Yugoslav policy recognizes the people of Slovenia as a nationality and a nation, and has given the nation status as one of Yugoslavia's six constituent republics. The country has also given Bosnia-Hercegovina republic status but according to current thought does not recognize the inhabitants as a single people or the political unit as a nation.[21] And lastly, Kosovo as an autonomous region within Serbia, does not enjoy republic status even though its Albanian inhabitants are recognized as a people, and even further as a nationality.[22] Therefore, the use of nation and nationality in their traditional conceptions can only add to the complexity present in Yugoslavia. Hence, the term nation-building will not be used in this analysis to describe the wider, Yugoslav building process.

The third reason for avoiding the traditional conception of the term nation and nation-building results from the emotionalism that the term conveys and the political nerves that it touches in the country. To speak openly of "Yugoslav" nation-building is to speak of "Yugoslavism" which inevitably raises the emotions of the advocates of republic identity.[23] Although the idea might be perceived as rather innocuous by a foreign observer, the idea and possibility of the slow dissolution of one's language, national heritage, and culture is inevitably perceived with concern by many natives upon hearing one speak of a Yugoslav nation and nation-building. Therefore, the term nation-building is not only misleading and extremely complicated in the Yugoslav context, but also is an unacceptable expression in current Yugoslav parlance.

Other terms are available and perhaps could be used with more clarity in the Yugoslav setting. For example, one could talk about the state or "state-building." However, state seems to be an unacceptable term given both its classical, its contemporary, and its legalistic conceptions. Its classical conception is unacceptable because it implies a total homogeneity of parts, a homogeneity that certainly does not exist in the Yugoslav context, and furthermore, is unlikely to be attained in the future. Graham speaks of the classical conception in the following manner:

> A State . . . must be a homogeneous "nation," because no citizen can imagine his State or make it the object of his political affection unless he believes in the existence of a national type to which the individual inhabitants of the State are assimilated; and he cannot continue to believe in the existence of such a type unless in fact his fellow-citizens are like each other and like himself in certain important respects.[24]

The ethnic-religious and cultural heterogeneity in Yugoslavia makes the desirability and likelihood of assimilation to a national type very remote for the present. There is so much variation of characteristics in Yugoslav life, that "fellow citizens" often find themselves demonstrating more contrasting than common attributes. At the same time, this should not, and of course, does not rule out the possibility of some sort of process of assimilation and a greater homogeneity in the future.[25]

A more modern conception of state and that incidentally in current usage in Yugoslavia reserves the term for a narrower meaning, i.e., the sovereign political unit possessing power within the international sphere. For example, if a Yugoslav ambassador were to refer to his country, he would use the term Yugoslav state. Karl Deutsch, similarly, uses the term "nation-state" to refer to a nation that has become sovereign through the inauguration of a new or old state organization.[26] Finally, the term state in its contemporary usage is excessively constitution or organization focused and too mechanistic for our purposes since the study is less concerned with the constitutional, structural nature of Yugoslavia than with the human processes of communication, cooperation, and understanding. The term is, therefore, not of any real value for this study since the classical conception refers to a homogeneous unity not particularly appropriate to present-day Yugoslavia, and the contemporary sense tends to denote a sovereign constitutional regime and ignores the human features of the society.

For purposes of this study, then, another term will be employed to identify the human elements of the development process. First, Yugoslavia will be conceived of as the manifestation of a higher form of political experience. This form will be based upon a conception of Yugoslavia as a larger socialist community formed of a number of smaller nations (*nacije*) and peoples (*narod*). In Serbo-Croatian this conception might be defined in one of two ways depending upon one's personal orientation. *Jugoslovenska zajednica naroda* translates to mean "a Yugoslav community of peoples" and is preferred by the advocates of greater republic rights and autonomy. *Jugoslovenska socijalisticka zajednica* means "a Yugoslav socialist community" and has wider acceptance among the advocates of Yugoslav unity. This conception of Yugoslavia corresponds with official policy which argues that socialist values should be of greater importance than national and other "lower-order" elements. Edvard Kardelj, the Yugoslav's chief theoretician on the question, explained the idea in 1953 when he noted:

> All society's means for production are general people's property, that is in a practical sense the property of all workers in our country. This is a new factor which creates a socialist community of a new type in which language and national culture become a secondary factor.[27]

It would have been impossible to hold this conception of Yugoslavia before the Second World War for a number of more or less important reasons: first, the political realities of the inter-war years exacerbated the divisions created by different language and national cultures;[28] second, prior to World War II there was not the spiritual bond resulting from the shared Communist resistance movement that drew participants from throughout Yugoslavia and transcended more strictly national boundaries; third, there was not the common experience resulting from Yugoslavia's expulsion from the Cominform and the events following in the aftermath which forced the Yugoslavs to "go it alone;" fourth, there was not the contemporary, highly developed communications system that cuts across and binds the various regions of present-day Yugoslavia. Fifth, and probably the most important, there was not the thirty years of cooperation between the various nations within the framework of a socialist system that has allowed and enhanced the evolution of a common set of values, objectives, and aspirations that arise above more particularistic desires. These five factors allow us to conceive of Yugoslavia as a broader socialist community.[29]

There are good reasons for conceiving of Yugoslavia in this manner. Otto Bauer, the Austrian Socialist writer, notes that it is not the similarity of characteristics (e.g., language, nationality, etc.) that is so important to a country but rather the effects of a molding force or the experiences of a common history. That is, the difference between Slovene and Macedonian may be rather insignificant compared to the commonality experienced during the Partisan liberation movement and the events of the post-war years. Bauer distinguishes between a "similarity of character" and a deeper conception called a "community of character" in the following manner:

> While . . . similarity of character can only be observed in the majority of the members of the nation, the community of character, the fact that they are all the products of one and the same effective force, is common to all of them without exception. This effective force, that which is historical in us, is that which is national in us. It is this which welds us into a nation.[30]

According to Bauer's conception, then, Yugoslavia might be viewed as a higher form of "nation," that is, a community of character welded together by the historical experiences of the resistance movement and the important events following in the post-war years.

This notion conceives of the possibility of a transitional phase between the former national units and a higher form of political community. The ideas of Sturzo are relevant to this conception;

> Like all moral personalities, the nation will have its increment and development . . . until the national personality will either fade away because its physical subject has . . . nearly perished (as in the case of the Armenians and the Assyrians), or will be transferred to a larger and different personality, reviving in a broader circle of ethnical, cultural and political unity, as Montenegro in Yugoslavia.[31]

When coupling this kind of developmental logic with Marxist theory, the idea has significant relevance to the Yugoslav socialist community. The post-war regime has not been unaware of the potential of this blending of modernization logic with Marxist concepts to handle the particularistic tendencies of a multi-national state. In fact, Shoup implies that the regime placed great emphasis on the value changes brought about by social and economic change in addition to noting the importance of ideological and political formulas:

> In down-to-earth terms, the Yugoslavs hoped to create the conditions under which social change and economic progress would lead to a mixing of the nationalities and lessening of their parochial national outlooks (something along the lines of the American experience), rather than continuing to rely indefinitely on the revolutionary formulas and techniques of political indoctrination employed as a means of transforming national attitudes in the immediate post-war years.[32]

The Marxist prediction concerning the lessening of provincial outlooks and the heightening of socialist goals, coupled with the value change produced by social and economic progress, are both relevant aspects of the building of a broader socialist community in contemporary Yugoslavia. This study will focus, then, upon the latter aspect and conceive of Yugoslavia in terms of a larger socialist community constructed from a number of diverse nations and minority nationalities.

This notion of community implies a number of characteristics, one of them being communication. Deutsch notes, "when we say 'community' we stress the aspects of communication."[33] Communities are based upon the exchange of information and are directly dependent upon the facility of the exchange process. Where communication barriers exist, the exchange of information will be low and the likelihood of community growth to be limited. The traditional relations based upon more particularistic, provincial concerns can clearly be viewed as barriers to the exchange of symbols in the larger Yugoslav community. When relatively fewer or weaker barriers exist, the chances for community development are enhanced.

However, before arriving at the particular conception of community to be used in this study, it might be instructive to view some definitions of others.[34] Quincy Wright offers an organizational or mechanistic definition of community. He writes: "The word 'community' refers to the organization of all social entities, in direct or indirect contact with one another, within an area."[35] Elsewhere he notes:

A community differs from other forms of association in including the entire population of an area. A perfect community is objectively one which manifests cultural uniformity, spiritual union, institutional unity, and material unification in the highest possible degree and subjectively one with which the members resemble one another closely in evaluations, purposes, understandings, appreciations, prejudices, appearances, and other characteristics which any of them consider important. They are all in continuous contact with group sentiment, contributing to group policy and accepting group decisions. The government of such a community is capable of preserving peace and justice within it and of assuring cooperation of the members in its constitutionally accepted policies. Such a community supplies all the needs of its members and is self-sufficient and isolated.[36]

And then, in a sentence that is extremely relevant to this study, he adds:

A community is not a nation if different individuals within it identify themselves primarily with different groups, some with a church, some with a class, others with a family, or village.[37]

The study herein views this phenomenon of identification in terms of degree. That is, Yugoslavia may be viewed as a community to the extent or degree to which members of the citizenry detach themselves from such particularistic objects. This conception permits one to view the phenomenon in a change perspective. As identification with more provincial and particularistic attachments declines, the community can be viewed as in a process of growth. As the strength of such attachments increases, the Yugoslav socialist community might be conceived as in a state of decline.

Deutsch defines community in a similar fashion: "Community consists of people who have learned to communicate with each other and to understand each other well beyond the mere interchange of goods and services."[38] Deutsch maintains that communities are dependent upon the exchange of information and the understanding that this information may bring. Then, however, it seems reasonable that the idea of community will imply something deeper to the people who compose it. Basically, it implies a sense of cooperation among the participating, component parts. This study will use these three phenomena—communication, understanding, and cooperation—to trace the likelihood, development, and future of community in the Yugoslav state.

Specifically, by evaluating the attributes and value systems of the Yugoslav citizenry, as well as those of the representatives of different sub-groups within the larger citizenry, this study will attempt to judge whether or not the individuals are equipped to engender these three aspects of community. If the overall citizenry and various sub-groups within the larger population are equipped with a certain set of social attributes and value configurations, then communication, cooperation, and understanding may be facilitated and the chances for community enhanced. However, the relative absence of these individual, facilitating characteristics may be such to diminish the likelihood of community within the Yugoslav context.

Even though the term community will be used predominantly throughout the study, it may still be convenient at times to refer to Yugoslavia as a single nation, as is often done by many non-Yugoslav scholars. Some contemporary conceptions of the term nation permit this type of conceptual interchange between nation and community. In his study *From Empire to Nation*, Rupert Emerson conceives of a nation as "a community of people who feel that they belong together in the double sense that they share deeply significant elements of a common heritage and that they have a common destiny for the future."[39] If this contemporary conception of nation is applied to the Yugoslav situation, it is possible to conceive of the larger socialist community as a nation. Although the analysis will use the term community for the larger part of the study, when the term nation is employed to refer to the Yugoslav "community of people," it is conceived of according to Emerson's definition.[40]

Some Dynamics of the Change Process[41]

The study envisions a model of the overall change process in Yugoslavia that is characterized by the following basic dynamics. Rapid economic progress has been evidenced in Yugoslavia over the post-war years. In an outstanding study of economic activity in Yugoslavia, Hamilton evaluates the progress in the following words:

> The government's postwar strategy has undoubtedly achieved outstanding economic progress. Real national income per capita in 1965 averaged some $480, which is four times as much as the estimated figure of $115 for 1938. Indeed, except for the years 1950-52, when the full impact of the Cominform blackage on the Yugoslavian economy abroad coincided with severe droughts which has disastrous effects on agriculture at home, the economy has been expanding at an average rate of 7 per cent per annum while a rate of growth of 13 per cent per annum, one of the highest in the world, was common-place between 1957 and 1960.[42]

This economic progress has been affecting the social characteristics of the country. The change can be seen in the growth of the more affluent sector of the country (the "middle class" of capitalist societies), in the increasing mobility of the population, and in the concentration of more inhabitants in the urban centers.[43] The modern technology and life accompanying industrialization are undoubtedly transforming what was before the Second World War a predominantly "peasant society."[44] Lerner contends that when countries industrialize, the citizenry becomes "physically, socially, and psychically" more mobile.[45] When reviewing another study of modernization in Turkey, Lerner notes: "The radius of the world in which the individual lives his daily life widens in proportion to the degree of contact with modern technology."[46] Industrial change, urbanization, and socio-economic development in general, bring about new societal phenomena.[47] The Yugoslav living in this relatively more technological, and one might even say, increasingly cybernetic society is characterized by higher education, exposure to the mass media, internal and external travel, and general geographical mobility;[48] in general, socio-economic development brings about a citizenry more exposed to information and communication stimuli. These changes, to be subsumed in this study under a variable called social mobilization, suggest changes in belief systems.

Belief systems of Yugoslavs, as all human beings, consist of a number of complex, more or less interrelated components.[49] Two components of these systems were originally considered by the author of central importance to the community-building process in Yugoslavia.[50] Their importance was judged on the basis of their apparent relationship to encouraging further communication, cooperation, and understanding in the Yugoslav context. In effect, they appeared to represent attitudes and values which might determine the growth or decline of community in the Yugoslav socialist state. The first configuration of values is found in the belief systems of individuals throughout the world and represents one's values along a modernized to traditional perspective.[51] The second value component, also of world-wide significance but also of special importance in the Yugoslav context, refers to the beliefs of an individual as evaluated along a universalistic to culturally particularistic dimension.[52] These two components were defined first through theoretical discussions and later identified through factor analysis of the survey data. After this general delineation, the values were evaluated and scored by the Guttman analysis procedure and provided two individual variables of central importance to studying the dynamics of the community-building process in present-day Yugoslavia.[53]

In summary, then, social and economic development is altering the social characteristics (to be referred to as the characteristics of social mobilization) of the Yugoslav citizenry. These changes imply alterations in the belief systems of the population. Finally, these mobilization characteristics and value alterations suggest important implications for the process of community-building. The basic variables in the model can be represented schematically in sequential form (See Figure 1). The study will not direct empirical consideration to the initial link between societal variables and social mobilization (Variable A). Statistical indicators published annually by the country have already shown that the two are correlates of the

FIGURE 1

VARIABLES IN THE CHANGE MODEL[a]

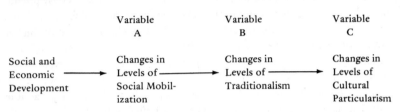

[a]This model certainly does not profess to include all of the variables relevant to the change process in Yugoslavia. It is not intended for that purpose. It only purports to delineate a general relationship between societal change and individual change; and then, to identify three separate aspects of individual change (represented by variables A, B, and C) of importance to the community-building process.

development process. However, the study will focus upon the relationships among the individual variables, dynamics that can be traced only by securing data that are not usually so accessible for analysis. Through cross-sectional analysis, the study will then consider whether or not a causal linkage exists among individual attributes A, B, and C. The existence or absence of this linkage within the Yugoslav citizenry will not only offer information about some current dynamics of the community-building process in the country, but on the basis of the projected proliferation of mobilization stimuli, will also offer predictions for the future. Furthermore, by viewing a number of sub-groups within the society, comparative information can be gained about the relative postures and rates of change among diverse social and national groups within the country.

Social mobilization is the most important variable in the chain due to the formulation which defines it as the initial causal factor in the sequence of "individual" variables. Karl Deutsch suggested such a factor having causal capabilities over a decade ago when he stated:

> Social mobilization is a name given to an overall process of change, which happens to substantial parts of the population in countries which are moving from traditional to modern ways of life. It denotes a concept which brackets together a number of more specific processes of change, such as changes of residence, of occupation, of social setting, of face-to-face associates. . . . Singly, and even more in their *cumulative impact*, these changes tend to influence and sometimes to transform political behavior.[54] (*Italics mine.*)

Deutsch therefore suggests that during periods of social change, certain processes are likely to occur within the individual which he contends "tend to influence" and possibly "transform" individual behavior. A causal mechanism is implicitly suggested in the conception of social mobilization, a mechanism which will later be used in this study to suggest the possible effect or influence of these phenomena upon elements of an individual's belief system. Namely, it will be *hypothesized* that the cumulative effect of the various processes of change brought together under the social mobilization factor tend to engender more modern and less particularistic value configurations within the Yugoslav populace. It will also be hypothesized that this process of individual change tends to equip the individual with resources conducive to the further development of community in the socialist Yugoslav state.

In summary, it has been suggested that economic development and ensuing changes in the social characteristics of the country are bringing about a higher level of social mobilization within the Yugoslav citizenry. These characteristics of mobilization, in turn, may be found to engender, first, a more modernized, and second, a less particularistic set of values within members of this citizenry. Then, as will be explained in a more elaborate fashion in Chapter 3, it may be argued that a mobilized, modernized, and non-particularistic set of attributes encourage the communication, cooperation, and understanding vital to the further development of community in a complex multi-national system such as the Yugoslav.

C. *Importance of Community-Building in the Yugoslav Setting*

Obstacles to development in all societies, and particularly in those commonly referred to as "transitional" or "developing" societies, are extensive and varied. There are problems of external or foreign interference in domestic affairs, of shortages in material and human resources, and of inabilities in employing these limited resources in productive manners. These kinds of manifest problems are more easily seen and studied by interested scholars. However, there is also another important domestic problem of relevance to the development process, that which is identified here as community-building. This issue is not so easily recognized and considerably more difficult to study; hence, it has often been overlooked or lightly treated. The issue of community-building reflects the human aspects of the development process, aspects which present basic problems in Yugoslavia that must be dealt with in the interests of further development.

The Yugoslav system presents a particularly relevant and appropriate societal setting in which to study community-building because of two primary factors: first, the presence of a relatively parochial citizenry that historically reacted rather hesitantly toward social and political integration, and second, the presence of diverse lingual, religious, and national cultures within its boundaries. Due to the overlapping and reinforcing nature of these language, religion, and nationality characteristics, rather homogeneous and cohesive sub-cultures have survived within the specific geographical regions making up the larger Yugoslav state. This geographical proximity coupled with an intense pride in one's cultural distinctness has given continuing sustenance to the historical particularism and nationalism existing in the heterogeneous South Slavic context. In short, the historical and contemporary composition of the Yugoslav state has been such to encourage traditionalism and cultural particularism rather than their desired (at least by the political leadership) counterparts—namely, modernization and political-cultural integration.

In an attempt to cope with this potentially disintegrative condition and the diversity of ethnic groupings existing within the state, the post-World War II regime followed a strategy of allowing, and even encouraging, cultural equality and autonomy while forcing economic development. In an effort to carry out this strategy, individual republics were granted to the various nationalities under the stipulations of the 1946 constitution. At the same time, the post-war regime called for the rapid development and modernization of the entire country which, in some instances, was perceived to be at the expense of the more developed regions.

The central question remains, however: has this strategy and ensuing economic development brought about a more modernized and less particularistic citizenry? If not, the basic restraints to the further construction of the Yugoslav system may remain even today. The problem is that the relatively low level of modernization and the extremely heterogeneous composition of Yugoslavia aggravate the basic problems of traditionalism and cultural particularism. In so doing, these two factors continue to have restraining effects upon the functioning and evolution of the multi-national Yugoslav state. In effect, the Yugoslav system has been confronted with constructing a modern, socialist community out of a more traditional, "multi-national society." The social and political relevance and implications of this problem should be clear. Basically, what is at issue is whether culturally diverse, and yet geographically related and intermixed peoples can find ways of living cooperatively within the joint enterprise of a federated political system. No matter how one wishes to evaluate the Yugoslav strategy, it should be recognized that their efforts at handling the domestic relations between what have often proven to be divisive, particularistic groups could become a model for many of the newly developing nations of Africa and Asia.

In one of his works Deutsch approaches the crux of the problem confronting Yugoslavia and these other countries when he asks, "Just what do we mean when we say that . . . a social and political attachment to a small ethnic, cultural, or linguistic group has been overcome in the process of national integration?"[55] He subsequently answers that question:

> Open or latent resistance to political amalgamation into a common national state; minimal integration to the point of passive compliance with the orders of such an amalgamated government; deeper political integration to the point of active support for 'such a common state but with continuing ethnic or cultural group cohesion and diversity; and finally the coincidence of political amalgamation and integration with the assimilation of all groups to a common culture—these could be the main stages on the way from tribes to nation. However, since a nation is not an animal or vegetable organism, its evolution need not go through any fixed sequence of these steps.[56]

The sequence that any developing social system evolves through is usually uncharted and often complex. This is particularly true in the case of the Yugoslav. However, in this study attention will be addressed to what might be called the "Yugoslav sequence," an evolutionary sequence which the author contends does not necessarily coincide with the pattern described by Deutsch.

D. The Theoretical Bases: Background of the Problem

It may be instructive to view the problem within the frame of past and on-going research. Of the existing studies, only those will be reviewed which are felt to be of the most pressing significance. The first, published as *The Passing of Traditional Society: Modernizing the Middle East*, resulted from the research carried out by the Bureau of Applied Social Research of Columbia University during the years of 1950 and 1951.[57] The Bureau conducted a total of 1,600 extensive interviews with individuals from Iran, Egypt, Turkey, Syria, Lebanon, and Jordan. The project was intended to gather information concerning the exposure of the respondents to communication stimuli, and furthermore, personal attitudes as related to questions of political and social change.

In the major publication resulting from this project, Daniel Lerner viewed the process of modernization in the six countries as occurring in three historical phases:

> Urbanization comes first, for cities alone have developed the complex of skills and resources which characterize the modern industrial economy. Within this urban matrix develop both of the attributes which distinguish the next two phases—literacy and media growth.[58]

"Such a dynamic," he contends, "must connect institutional changes with alterations in the prevailing personal style."[59] He hypothesizes that the

individual who lives through the changes existent in this kind of environment becomes or assumes a "mobile personality." This personality, he
continues, provides the person with a capacity to identify with the new
aspects of his environment, and this is "the predominant personal style
only in modern society, which is distinctively industrial, urban, literate,
and participant."[60]

This study of Yugoslavia focuses on a similar type of dynamic and is
perhaps no less complex, even though it is dealing with one state, in place
of Lerner's six. That is, the conception must still take into account the
diversity that exists across Yugoslavia. While being cognizant of this diversity, the model assumes that economic change in Yugoslavia—although of
course varied—is bringing about a change of social characteristics (i.e., a
more highly educated, exposed, and traveled citizenry) and that a dynamic
exists between this social and economic change and the change within
"men's mind." The model acknowledges the basic setting that Lerner has
charted. After reviewing the economic indicators of Yugoslavia, it accepts
as fact that the country is indeed undergoing rapid urbanization and industrialization; then, within this state of economic and social change, it will
attempt to investigate the social-psychological dynamics characterizing the
individual, and furthermore, the relationship they appear to have to the
process of community-building.

Another important study, the Almond-Verba "Five-Nation Study" of
democratic development, addressed itself to this general question, although the basic published work, *The Civic Culture*, showed little attempt
to investigate relationships among the different aspects of individual
change.[61] It was, however, an impressive effort to show variations in individual attitudes across five nations and set the stage for more sophisticated
analysis of the data. An impressive study that draws upon the Almond-
Verba data has been published in two parts as "Social Structure and Political Participation: Developmental Relationships, I and II."[62] This study
represents a rather successful attempt to causally link four basic phases
of the development process through the techniques of cross-sectional analysis. The authors hypothesize that economic development brings about
successive and cumulative alterations in the following aspects of the society:
(1) the stratification, urban, and group membership patterns of the population; (2) the distribution and composition of attitudes and cognitions
on the part of the citizenry, and; (3) the levels of political participation
of this same citizenry.[63] Again, the theory suggested in this re-analysis of
the Almond-Verba data has certain similarities to the one represented in
this study of Yugoslavia, but differs somewhat in its selection of variables.
Whereas Nie, Powell, and Prewitt selected the stratification, urban, and
group membership patterns (or more simply, social structure) as their

primary causal variable, this study selected a constellation of variables that relate more closely to the individual's exposure to communication stimuli and cultural contact. This study of Yugoslavia, then, hypothesized that economic development brings about successive and cumulative alterations in the following characteristics of the Yugoslav populace: (1) increases in the level of social mobilization, (2) decreases in the level of traditional values, (3) decreases in the level of particularistic values, (4) and increases in the likelihood for community development.

The study selected these variables only after considering the larger process of change in Yugoslavia. Changes in the social and economic life of the country were viewed as bringing about factors that were changing the individual. The problem at hand was to find out which social changes were most important in bringing about value change. After evaluating the effect of a large number of variables, it was decided that those surrounding the phenomenon of exposure to information were most significant.

There have been other works that have taken this general orientation. One of the most significant, Karl Deutsch's *Nationalism and Social Communication*, has drawn together a number of factors in an effort to operationalize some of the important aspects of change for quantitative treatment.[64] Deutsch has taken some basic concepts from a number of disciplines in the social sciences in order to build a structure that would lend itself to systematic inquiry. Basically, as the following quotation illustrates, all of the concepts he selected evolve around the notion of communication:

> Looking for such concepts, we may perhaps find them in the notion of communication. Processes of communication are the basis of the coherence of societies, cultures, and even of the personalities of individuals; and it may be worthwhile to see whether concepts of communication may not help us to understand the nature of peoples and of nations.[65]

Deutsch's theorizing about the influence of communication in mobilizing the population, in changing social habits and attitudes, and in modernizing and unifying political entities has had a significant impact upon the study of political change, political development, and community-building.

The research to be reported in this study, however, has one major point of departure from the conceptualizations and applications of Deutsch.[66] Whereas Deutsch focused upon the societal level of analysis and utilized aggregate data, this research focuses upon the individual level of analysis and utilizes survey data. While Deutsch analyzes levels of communication (newspapers read, travel, etc.) within large *social aggregates*, this study analyzes the same types of behavior at the individual level and assesses their influence upon the belief systems of individuals making up certain social aggregates. As a result, this study is able to go beyond the research of Deutsch in one important respect, into an area which few other researchers of community-building have gone.[67] Whereas Deutsch could only investigate relationships at the social level, and thus could not make inferences about the role of the individual in the community-building process without incurring the "ecological fallacy," individual data as used in this study, permit investigation of some important individual variables in the community-building process.[68]

One macro-project with this type of "micro-interest" has been conducted by Harvard's Center for International Affairs.[69] Through this project, entitled "Social and Cultural Aspects of Economic Development," 6000 citizens from six developing countries were interviewed to determine what factor or constellation of factors were of importance in "making men modern." Education, the researchers found, is the most powerful single factor in bringing about a modern personality. Inkeles suggests, however, that modernity is more than what is learned in school. It is also a battery of atttitudes and values relating to "man's orientation to nature, to time, to fate, to politics, to women, and to God."[70] As regards the impact of schools, Inkeles maintains:

> The effects of the school, I believe, reside not mainly in its formal, explicit, self-conscious pedagogic activity, but rather are inherent in the school as an *organization*. The modernizing effects follow not from its informal, implicit, and often unconscious program for dealing with its young charges. The properties of the rational organization as a hidden persuader—or, as I prefer to put it, as a silent and unobserved teacher—become most apparent when we consider the role of occupational experience in shaping the modern man.[71]

Therefore, Inkeles contends that exposure found through school and working organizations is of dominant importance in shaping the modern man.

The model developed in this study of Yugoslavia incorporates the variables utilized by Inkeles, and also adds some suggested and cited earlier by Deutsch. That is, the model to be emplyed here envisions a "mover" variable taking into account one's education, exposure to the mass media, and travel within and outside of the country. This grouping of variables has never been combined before to the knowledge of the author in order to trace the cumulative impact upon the individual. Data will be offered to show whether or not these variables tend to "set the individual in motion" within the Yugoslav context, and if so, whether they significantly alter his orientations toward such objects as his fellow man, his family, the supernatural, and fate. Then data will be examined to show whether this new configuration of values—which is said to be characteristic of the modern individual—significantly alters the individual's values relating to more provincial, particularistic attachments in the Yugoslav context. If so, we might have reason to contend that these individual changes are closely tied to the community-building process in the contemporary South Slavic state.

E. The Human Differences

Initially, and perhaps an instructive way to illustrate the nature of individual change taking place throughout Yugoslavia today is to view the nature of the change process characterizing some exemplary individuals. Later in the study, survey data will be employed to illustrate the nature of the phenomenon among the larger population. Before this larger study, however, it may be useful to relate my acquaintance with what might be called two "proto-typic" or "ideal types" met during my years in Yugoslavia. I would contend that the individual change taking place in the country today can be illustrated through the attributes and value systems of these two individuals—the first representing a young woman who was exposed and "open" to the earlier mentioned "causal" factors and the second representing the obverse.[72]

The first individual represents what might be called the "ideal-type" under analysis in the study. This person possessed the social characteristics and belief systems which are likely to be most conducive to the construction of a modern, unified political community. This well educated, widely traveled, and cultured individual once remarked:

> It isn't hard to explain the problems confronting our people when viewing our past. But our political history is not the only hindrance to our development, there is also the lack of cooperation and understanding among our peoples. Our people have to learn that the future of this country is hanging in the balance. If they will remain content to go about their traditional ways, and further, to prolong the disagreements among our people, then our chances in the modern world are very dim.

Because of the values expressed by this individual, I became extremely interested in the possible factors that had led to their formation. For while processing and analyzing statistically the Yugoslav survey data in the United States, I came across many of these "ideal-types" but was limited in the personal information that I could gather about them because of the unavoidable restrictions of a survey instrument. This, therefore, was a new experience that went beyond where the survey data itself had stopped.[73]

The first individual was a young graduate of one of Yugoslavia's best universities. Our acquaintance was made at the university and over the course of the year I was able to use our growing friendship as a new, albeit admittedly "unscientific," source of data.[74] We often talked about the process of change and community-building in Yugoslavia and about the role played by the individual. The values of the populace were often mentioned, as well as the likelihood of variations between different regions, and between different sectors in the same regions. Once I asked about the pattern of variations, and the cause and consequences of such variations, if they did in fact exist. A question of such scope is unfair to ask of anyone and particularly unfair to an inhabitant of a country representing the complexity found in Yugoslavia. However, the response was spontaneous and very direct. First, it was noted, the often-mentioned differences between the regions in Yugoslavia are undoubtedly present. The realities of foreign domination have probably not been without result. The influence ranges from the Turkish control of Macedonia, Bosnia-Hercegovina, and Serbia, to the Latin or Venetian control of the Dalmatian coast, and of course the centuries of Austro-Hungarian rule in Croatia and Slovenia. But did these years of foreign domination have an effect upon the values that I was interested in, for example, those concerning questions of traditionalism and particularism? Perhaps so, I was told; the Oriental or Turkish influence did introduce a style of life that was more personal in content and parochial in outlook. Concern for personal enjoyment, for visiting and singing with friends, is said to take on a central role in the lives of some of the inhabitants in the Turkish influenced areas. As a result, a rather different art or style of living seems to have developed in these areas. Some say that the acceptance of one's fate has characterized the population for centuries and note that it was probably this more "fatalistic" atttitude that made 500 years of Turkish domination possible. In short, it was being noted, emphasis on tradition, supernaturalism, fate, and familialism was likely to be stronger in certain regions of the country than in others. Even so, variations within each of these regions are not absent, for certain segments seem to be breaking away from this style of life and the belief systems that are synonymous with them. As I thought about these ideas, it seemed that it was not so much the cultural heritage (e.g., of the Turkish influenced areas) that was maintaining traditional and particularistic value systems today, but rather the greater isolation of certain people and groups from the information and stimuli that tend to bring about a modern life. Or stated differently, it may be unreasonable for one to expect a man to change from his past if he does not have some stimulus or reason for change. Some people were able to break from the isolation created by their parents' inability even to read, or to communicate, or in any way break outside of what was a relatively restricted information network. In the past, one's own village and family drew the predominance of the individual's working and leisure time. However, with the arrival of mass education, modern mass media, and the ability to travel throughout the country and oftentimes even to Italy, Austria, Germany and eastern countries, the individual has been given the opportunity to broaden his exposure. This opportunity, my friend noted, was bringing about a new kind of individual in Yugoslavia.

The dynamics of the change process had always deeply interested me. Was there any structure to the phenomena surrounding the individual as he moved from one style of life, or from one set of values, to another, or did such changes take a completely haphazard, unpredictable form? During one of our many conversations I asked my friend about the possibility of any ordering of the phenomena; I clearly remember the answer one morning while observing a not uncommon sight—peasant women working on the edge of a large and relatively modern city. Their presence and their work took on a special significance when compared with that of the urban dwellers. Also their peasant dress and working tools (scythes and wooden rakes) presented a striking contrast to the dress and work of my friend, who by appearance and abilities may have stepped out of a fashionable boutique or the Yugoslav Assembly. Moreover, the following remarks were directed at these peasant women and vividly illuminate basic human differences in the country today.

> How can we expect them to break away from their fatalistic attitudes, their primary concern for their family, and their overall traditional belief systems. Their life from dawn to dusk is little more than their daily work and their daily conversations include only their co-workers. After the working day is completed they return to their homes, tired and exhausted, but happy to spend a few private hours with their families. Change of attitudes in such a world is almost nonexistent. These peasant women represent the same values that their parents held, and their children will also if they can not break the cycle. Furthermore, and what is most discouraging is that these people view their relations and our country from a very closed and narrow perspective. First, it is only their families that matter, and then their own friends, region and ethnicity. They are afraid and against that which is unknown and this is indeed sad because there is much that they do not know about our own country. As a result they are caught up in a system of private concerns, unable to view our country in a manner that will bring about a new Yugoslavia.

As we continued to watch the peasants go about their work in an atmosphere that I personally could not help interpreting as pleasant and content, I noticed that my friend had become irritated. I later realized that it bothered this young woman a great deal to stand by helplessly and watch women of her own country live, work, and—oddly enough to her—perhaps enjoy such a style of life. For it was this traditional style and lack of contact which this young citizen reasonably viewed as a restraint to the modernization and development of the Yugoslav state. How, my friend probably thought to herself, can we progress when large sectors of our population are controlled by a traditional and particularist spirit? And when such a spirit is present, how can they understand that the future of our complex and diverse country lies in the ability of each of us to know, understand, and cooperate with the other segments of our population? Clearly, she had good reason for her uneasy feeling when viewing the workers from this perspective.

Later in the year I came to know her better. She had been born shortly after the War, the daughter of two participants in the Partisan liberation movement. Her mother and father met during these difficult war years while fighting for the idea of a new Yugoslavia. Their marriage represented the existence of this new experiment for one was of Serbian background and the other Croatian. Their daughter was raised, therefore, not only in a "multi-national" country, but perhaps more significantly, in a "multi-national" household. She graduated with high marks from a Yugoslav university and now is holding a position consistent with her capabilities. The atmosphere created by her parents' emphasis on education, travel, and culture brought about a very modern and "open" individual.

Later in the year I met a contrasting personality, a woman who could have easily been one of those seen earlier working in traditional peasant dress. We met while observing the traditional peasant "cooking" of the famous Yugoslav brandy (*šlivovica*). The setting was a peasant family's courtyard in an area rather isolated from the city. My friendship with the family grew over the year and represented a marked and often refreshing contrast to our usual acquaintances in the cities. The husband and wife of this family had seen the crumbling of the Austro-Hungarian empire from the same plot of ground that they were living and working on to the present day. They had been unaffected by the highly charged inter-war years but maintained that they knew which side was "in the right." They had managed to avoid direct involvement in the war for "personal reasons" and were concerned more for themselves, their family, and "their" nation than for the idea of Yugoslavia. The head of the household once remarked:

> How could I gain by fighting? What would it have meant to me and my family? We would have lost on either side. And now "they" expect me to fall for the new ideas of togetherness, and brotherhood and community. It will never work. I can't understand how "they" expect the quarreling and struggling of centuries to be wiped away by the new ideas of today. I can only go on living with what I have. And that I can trust, but the new ideas will have to be proven.

How could one expect this family to participate in "new ideas" when they possessed little opportunity to understand them? How could these individuals think in terms of and participate in a "broader socialist community" when they had little idea of whom it includes and what it represents? It seemed that their apparent inability to comprehend could be traced to both the quantity and quality of the information they received. First, the quantity was extremely limited. They were unable to read, they had no radio or television, seldom traveled, and in general had little access to information outside of their immediate surroundings. Second, the quality of the information was very much determined by its source. It is not unlikely that they heard about and discussed the war only with very close friends and relatives living in the same village. They were getting the same information they had heard many times before. In short, it would be unreasonable to accuse them for holding "backward" beliefs and particularistic orientations when little opportunity or possibility existed for thinking otherwise.

Research on the individual has shown that any decision, attitude, or statement is based upon available information. One of the most basic, universal propositions of the social sciences is that values are learned and not inherited or inborn.[75] The beliefs of these individuals were the result of incoming stimuli, just as the calculations of a modern computer are the result of incoming data. Since this couple's education, exposure to the mass media, and contact with the outside world were minimal, they based their beliefs on what information they had at their disposal. Toward the unknown they exhibited a feeling of negativism, pessimism, and powerlessness. Furthermore, their orientations toward unknown objects and peoples within their own country could be described as provincial and particularistic. Clearly, this husband and wife represented perfectly contrasting characteristics when compared to the other friend mentioned above.

Soon this couple and the "old class" will pass away. The important question is directed toward the future. What happens then? Can these short accounts of two personal friendships be used to infer a larger country-wide trend? Scientifically, of course, they can not. However, the survey data to be analyzed in later chapters point to the accounts' relevance to some aspects of individual change taking place in the society. The influences of increased education, exposure to the mass media, and domestic and foreign travel are changing the post-war "peasant" society and in what seems to be an identifiable pattern. Before the war, the historical and cultural differences of the South Slavs impeded the communication, cooperation, and understanding on which a large community is dependent. Now, however, it may be found that the social and psychological concomitants of an industrializing, socialist society are working to transcend the former barriers which worked to restrict the evolution of a larger South Slav community in the past.

The author's acquaintance with the two exemplary individuals indicates that some individuals possess the attributes and values that engender communication, cooperation, and understanding among the South Slav peoples, while others do not. This study will direct itself to an investigation of the phenomena and change dynamics that are likely to bring about this set of characteristics, and then, to the relationships between these characteristics and the community-building process.

CHAPTER III

CONCEPTUALIZING THE RELATIONSHIP BETWEEN INDIVIDUAL CHANGE AND COMMUNITY-BUILDING

A. *Introduction*

An awareness of the historical, cultural, and environmental cleavages characterizing Yugoslavia gives some idea of the difficult task facing the post-war Titoist leadership. The leadership element, however, did not approach the task of community-building without a definite strategy in mind. By blending Marxist principles with modernization logic, the new regime hoped to create a different individual, a new socialist man, who would find it easier to transcend the divisions of the past. This process of individual change, the leaders reasoned, could be effected through a new ideological and environmental order which would be brought about by the social, political, and economic changes of the post-war Communist system.

The study at hand seeks some explanation of the process of individual change occurring within this environmental order, and then, an understanding of the effect of the change phenomena on the process of community-building. A major problem encountered in this kind of study is selecting a strategy for viewing, and a framework for conceptualizing, the individual change that bears upon the process of community-building. The first part of this problem was approached by using survey data gathered from almost 1200 Yugoslavs. These data provided the basic information needed to view the individual within the changing Yugoslav environment. The second problem was approached by identifying three basic attributes of the individual. These attributes were selected on the basis of their alleged importance to the construction of a larger community in present-day Yugoslavia. The first part of the problem, therefore, is basically a question of *research method* and *data collection*, while the second is one of *conceptualization*.

B. *Methodology*

Survey research is extremely useful in providing information about the attributes, value systems, and behavior of individuals. If a researcher, for example, is interested in knowing whether an individual travels extensively, or whether he feels it important to communicate with individuals of different thoughts and backgrounds, he can ask questions designed to gather this kind of information. This study needed similar kinds of information drawn from a sample representing the entire country-wide population. Therefore, data will be employed that were gathered by trained interviewers working for a professional research institute in Belgrade who interviewed 1186 Yugoslavs from all sections of the country.[1]

The question of sampling was no less important for the study than that of interviewing. In that regard, a modified form of stratified random sampling was employed in twenty-four systematically selected communes. Furthermore, a quota sample of approximately fifty interviewees was filled in each of the communes. The quotas to be filled in each commune were determined according to a defined proportion of occupational subgroups desired from all twenty-four communes. Hence, a pre-determined number of agricultural, industrial, professional, political, administrative, and educational interviewees were randomly selected according to accepted sampling procedures. This quota method controlled, in effect, for occupational role across the various communes. Such a procedure was necessary in order to achieve balance between the rural communes (predominance of peasant, agricultural occupations) and the highly urban communes (predominance of professional occupations). On the basis of this sample, 1186 interviewees were selected to which the survey instrument was administered.

In addition to dividing up the population into occupational strata, with samples taken from every stratum, another method called *cluster* or *area* sampling was employed. That is, instead of drawing the 1186 interviewees from throughout all of Yugoslavia, twenty-four areas (communes) were selected to reflect the range of national-cultural divisions in the country, as well as the range in levels of economic development. The final array of communes selected from these divisions represented every republic within Yugoslavia and at least three different levels of development within each republic. Thus, when properly controlled, the findings can be generalized to all culture-regions within Yugoslavia, to all levels of economic development, and to many other sub-populations within the country.

C. Conceptual Framework

The conceptualization of individual change requires data that correspond with the Yugoslavs' developmental logic—namely, that rapid ideological, social, and economic development will generate individual characteristics and value sets conducive to the evolution of a dynamic, integrated socialist community. Therefore, the concern in this study is to select data from the survey instrument that are logically and empirically related to the further development of this form of political and social experience. Hence, it is necessary to ascertain what it is about a man that helps engender such a community and what human characteristics militate against its evolution. Is the peasant who never leaves his isolated village likely to foster the communication upon which communities are based? Furthermore, will he tend to think and act as a member of this new and higher political form, or do his characteristics operate against such tendencies? Further, what values are characteristic of a member of this new community, and how are they related to further communication, cooperation, and understanding within the Yugoslav setting?

As noted above, for purposes of this study, community will refer to a grouping of individuals who have learned to communicate with, cooperate with, and understand one another. Although it would obviously be difficult to operationalize the three terms, it is not unreasonable to contend that certain individual characteristics and values are conducive to their realization. Namely, although it would be difficult to ascertain whether a people "had learned to communicate with each other," it would not be unrealistic to contend that certain characteristics engender such behavior. This is empirically possible and can be thought of in the following manner. The process of communication is dependent upon two main factors: facilities and behavior. The general socio-economic trends outlined in the previous chapter, as well as what is already known about the development of information flow in Yugoslavia, suggest that the facilities are becoming increasingly efficient.[2]. However, what about the use of these facilities? This audience response pattern is of prime importance to the idea of community. If the people are using their facilities—that is, if they are reading, listening, traveling, and watching—then they are participating in a community of complementary habits and behaviors.[3] Such participants are likely to be reading complementary newsprint, viewing the same country-wide television network, and in general, exposing themselves to similar kinds of information stimuli.

At this point it may be instructive to view another community of peoples who are characterized by internal heterogeneity similar to that of the Yugoslavs. A prime example is the case of the Swiss. Differentiated even more than the Yugoslavs by lingual, cultural, and geographical barriers, they are still commonly thought of as members of a distinct political community. Accordingly, it is quite evident that they have been and are currently using their communication facilities. As a result, they have created some of the common characteristics of a people within an integrated political-territorial unit, that is, characteristics that transcend some of the differences associated with language and nationality. Obviously, today the Swiss can be characterized by a higher level of community than the Yugoslavs, but it should also be noted that their experience at communicating, cooperating, and understanding goes back considerably further and developed under more favorable conditions than the Yugoslav.

Although indicators are available to tell something about communication and exposure to information stimuli in Yugoslavia, these alone are not enough. Conceivably, a person could have access to large amounts of information and be communicating extensively within the Yugoslav context, but still not be understanding or cooperating. Therefore, the conceptions of these two terms must be clarified within the investigation and then combined with the concept of communication. For purposes of the study, understanding will denote a mental process defined by a high capacity for viewing and explaining world and human relations in a rational, intelligible manner.[4] Lerner's study suggested that the "traditional" man could not conceive of thinking about world or nation-wide questions. This study will contend that the traditionalistic man in Yugoslavia also has such difficulties in approaching issues concerning interpersonal, inter-ethnic, and international relations. Cooperation within the Yugoslav context, in turn, is a mental process defined by a capacity for transcending particularistic concerns in the pursuit of common problems. The study will contend that such behavior is unlikely when an individual is controlled by the constrictive nature of a particularistic set of values.

At this point it is necessary to shift from conceptual terms to operational variables. In that regard, this study will maintain that community in the complex Yugoslav environment is more likely to exist among a mobilized, modernized, and non-particularistic citizenry. This type of citizenry is more likely to be equipped with the resources necessary to communicate, understand, and cooperate in the Yugoslav context. Community-building in Yugoslavia, then, can be conceptualized and measured by viewing the levels of, as well as the relationships among, social mobilization, traditionalism, and cultural particularism within the citizenry of that state. Furthermore, by making the same assessment among a number of different sub-sectors within the society, some comparative insights into the dynamics of the process should be found.

Before moving into a specific discussion of each of these three attributes, the inter-relationships among them, and the theoretical and empirical underpinnings for suggesting such relationships, it might be useful to direct discussion to each since they have rather varied uses within the social sciences. The first variable, social mobilization, refers to a characteristic of the individual which describes the extent of his contact, exposure to, and communication with other members and segments of his society.[5] Deutsch describes this variable in the following terms:

> Within any geographical setting and any population, economic, social, and technological developments mobilize individuals for

relatively more intensive communication. We may call this the
social and political public, or the *mobilized population*, and we
may delimit this mobilized population (i.e., population mobilized
for mass communication) by various yardsticks of measurements;
the set of persons who live in towns: the set of persons engaged in
occupations other than agriculture, forestry, and fishing; the set of
persons who read a newspaper at least once a week . . . . Together
(these sets) might well serve to indicate the public or the mobilized
population.[6]

In this study, the mobilized population will be delimited by similar "yardsticks" of measurements, with each "yardstick" representing an ordinal
level variable upon which the respondents are individually evaluated. Each
of the 1186 individuals will be characterized according to:

a) level of education (seven categories ranging from low to high)

b) level of exposure to radio, television, and newspapers (three categories ranging from low to high exposure)

c) extent of internal travel (nine categories ranging from low to high)

d) extent of external travel (five categories ranging from low to high)

These four items were used to construct a summated scale which assessed
(or delimited) each individual along an ordinal index ranging from low
levels to high levels of mobilization.

The second variable, modernism-traditionalism, refers to a component
of an individual's belief system that is made up of a number of value prem-
ises.[7] This variable is similar to Lerner's "modernization" which he speaks
of as "the infusion of a rationalist and positivist spirit."[8] Implicit in the
scale are a number of value dimensions which were represented by five
evaluative statements taken from the survey instrument. The statements,
which evaluate the emphasis and importance placed on tradition, super-
naturalism, fate, familialism, negativism and the lack of rationalism, were
Guttman analyzed to form a unidimensional scale laboeled modernism.[9]
Each of the respondents were then assigned a value on this scale to represent the individual's posture along a dimension ranging from low to high
modernism.[10]

The third major variable, cultural universalism-particularism, has special
application in a society historically characterized by high levels of cultural
pluralism and heterogeneity. Within most societies, elements are present
that have a tendency, or at least a capability, for separating people along a
number of potentially disintegrative lines. These elements represent potential barriers to the behaviors and values that bind political communities.
Examples are race or social class in the United States, nationality in Europe, language in Canada and Belgium, regionalism in the Congo or Vene-
zuela, and religion and custom in India. Cleavages along such lines form a
basis for particularism, and in the case of Yugoslavia, a number of these

potential sources are present. Therefore, in an area characterized by the extreme ethnic and cultural pluralism of Yugoslavia, the third component is especially relevant. In other words, the Yugoslav socialist community is particularly susceptible to barriers based upon the ethnic and cultural attachments called "cultural differentiators" by Anderson, von der Mehden, and Young, and "primordial attachments" by Shils and Geertz.[11] Their analyses, as will this study, point to potential foci from which the problems of particularism result.

The problem of cultural particularism is basically a question of the focus for an individual's attachments, identifications, and loyalties in the modern nation-state. The Yugoslavs, without question, have been and are today confronted by problems that result from the individual's identification with "lower-level" particularistic elements. These elements have had the tendency of impeding communication, understanding, and cooperation within the country. In effect, they have created invisible barriers or boundaries within the generalized state system.[12] The general strength of identification with such elements, however, varies significantly from individual to individual. It is this variation of course that suggests the usefulness of the Universalism-Particularism scale upon which every respondent can be evaluated on a number of possible, particularistic elements.

The universalism variable is represented by a Guttman scale constructed from five evaluative statements taken from the survey instrument.[13] Each statement reflects a different particularistic object or attachment that exists in the Yugoslav context. Therefore, when the study speaks of cultural universalism or particularism in Yugoslavia, it refers to the presence or absence of patterns of identification that stem from one or more of the following five sources:

a) *National or Ethnic Identification*: The first dimension of particularism in Yugoslavia may be thought of as a sense of national identification which has been evolving historically for centuries within this area in the Balkans. Within the distinct nations and nationalities of Yugoslavia there is a sense of commonality that is centered around one's culture, one's ancestry, one's common history, and set of traditions.

b) *Language*: The second may be seen as an element of linguistic identity which is of major importance in the Yugoslav context.[14] Besides the three major recognized languages of Serbo-Croatian, Slovenian, and Macedonian, there are numerous minority languages and regional dialects that also represent factors creating potential sources of linguistic cleavage within the larger state.

c) *Region or Locale*: The third criterion, regionalism or localism, is a prime source of attachment and identity for the individual in geographically heterogeneous areas such as Yugoslavia. It is a factor that involves the

nationality and language criteria but represents a socio-political and economic dimension that is distinct. Namely, the commune and republic within
Yugoslavia represent governmental units of special importance to the individual. The attachment of the individual to these units, therefore, reveals
a potentially particularistic concern illustrating distinctiveness in social,
cultural, economic and political issues.

d) *Family*: Although a basis for identification nearly everywhere, the
family in Yugoslavia has special relevance because of its solidarity through
South Slavic history.[15] Although relatively few exist today, the historical
tradition and nature of the *zadruga*, being formed on the basis of a biologi-
cal relationship, still creates a source commanding personal identification
in the country. Numerous studies of cultural change have pointed to the
dis-integration of the family unit with the development of a modern
nation-state.[16] This is no less true in Yugoslavia. Those who place greater
importance upon family concerns are less likely to possess the characteristics conducive to the development of a modern socialist community.

e) *Values and Norms*: Differences in value orientations and behavior
patterns also form a basis for potential cleavage and fragmentation within
any state, Yugoslavia in particular. The different value systems found in
the diverse regions, and the attachments they create, when coupled with
the basic differences caused by religion and ethnicity, give rise to potential
obstacles impeding integrative trends.

Taken together, these five possible sources for psychological attachment form an ideal Guttman scale that can be used to assess the relative
level of universalism and particularism of each of the respondents. It
would be impossible to accurately evaluate the level by considering only
one of these five possible sources. However, by asking all 1186 individuals
a set of five questions, it is possible to obtain a score representing the degree of an individual's "sub-community" loyalties.[17] By asking the 1186
individuals about the importance of each of the possible sources of loyalty, it was possible to rank the various attachments in terms of their relative
importance.[18] While being cognizant of the varied phrasing of the evaluative statements, the marginals show the following range from most important to least important: family, language or dialect, nationality, locale, and
value system. That is, Yugoslavs are very closely attached to their families,
but at the same time, are rather open to communication with individuals
representing opposing value positions.[19] Separately, the attachments yield
rather limited information about the individual; however, when taken together and Guttman analyzed, they yield thirty-one unique scores by
which each of the 1186 individuals can be analyzed.

After having operationalized these three basic variables, is there any
theoretical and empirical basis for assuming some sort of relationship

between and among them, and if so, what does it mean to the overall community-building process? First, when directing attention toward the relationships between the three attributes of the individual, it seems logical to hypothesize an ordering among the three on the basis of what is known from other studies of the modernization process. That is, when a person becomes more mobilized, it theoretically follows and empirically has been shown, that he will tend to become less traditional. Accordingly, the landmark studies of both Lerner and Inkeles showed that a man more exposed to communication stimuli is a man more modern in his beliefs.[20] The effect of the mobilization variable has everyday application within the quickly changing Yugoslav environment. The movement of formerly "isolated" people to the cities, their taking a job in a modern factory, and then possibly attending one of the Workers' Universities (i.e., adult education programs), provide good examples illustrating this point. This rapid change, as well as other accompanying changes such as mass media exposure and greater interpersonal contact, expose the individual to a different style of life. He is learning new things, interacting with new people, and generally finding himself exposed to a broader range of information stimuli. As a result, it would be reasonable to expect that his value system will also change.

With this increasing in-take of communication stimuli, and the resulting tendency to form more modern beliefs, the individual may become less attached to the personalized, particularistic loyalties of a traditional life.[21] As the earlier-mentioned individual moves to the city and assumes a life style representative of the more modern setting, he may find his traditional loyalties to locale, family, dialect, and so on, increasingly coming into question. His reference groups may change, he forms new friendships, and in general, is likely to find himself spatially and psychologically removed from his former, more parochial attachments. As a result, he is likely to become less affected by them.[22]

Therefore, after having closely examined the Yugoslav's developmental logic, the changing Yugoslav context and the posture of the individual within this context, and after having closely surveyed past research on the question, hypotheses can now be offered for the purpose of empirical research. These hypotheses will subsequently be used to determine whether a patterned and identifiable relationship exists between and among the three variables. The relationships to be investigated can be described in hypothesis form:

1. If levels of social mobilization increase, then levels of modernism will tend to increase.
2. If levels of social mobilization increase, then levels of cultural universalism will tend to increase.

3. If levels of modernism increase, then levels of cultural universalism will tend to increase.

Other hypotheses are of course conceivable and will be investigated in the analysis of the data. For example, is it theoretically possible and do the data point to individuals who are of high mobilization and modernism levels, and at the same time, at low levels of universalism? Or another conceivable example, are there individuals who represent relatively low levels of mobilization but who are also extremely modern and non-particularistic? These are of course possibilities and will receive consideration in the ensuing chapters. However, the three hypotheses listed here represent the "optimal" or "ideal-typical" evolution of characteristics, an evolution seemingly most conducive to the further development of a country-wide form of community within the Yugoslav state. The relationships can be illustrated in diagram form with the ordinal numbers identifying the hypothesized linkages (see Figure 2).

FIGURE 2
ARROW DIAGRAM REPRESENTING THE CONCEPTUALIZATION OF INDIVIDUAL CHANGE

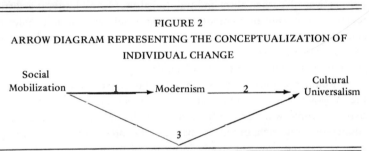

In summary, it is hypothesized that a cumulative ordering and sequential relationship may exist across the three variables. As an individual becomes more mobilized, he in turn is likely to become more modern in his beliefs. Then after possessing this set of characteristics, his values are likely to become more universalistic within the Yugoslav context.[23]

At this juncture it is necessary to consider further whether there is any reason to assume that the three characteristics of the individual and the hypothesized relationships among them have any effect on the overall community-building process. The question is best addressed in the following manner. Community-building as a process may be identified as the development of mobilization, modernization, and universalistic characteristics among the inhabitants of any political-territorial unit. One can not say that Yugoslavia, or any other society for that matter, is a totally developed community. However, one can rank any number of states according to the presence of the community-building characteristics among various sectors of their populace.

It would be difficult to conceive of a large, modern community binding such diverse peoples as Slovenes, Albanians, and Macedonians if large sectors of the society could not read, and further, if they were isolated from one another and immobile: the very idea of community is based upon the contact of ideas and peoples.[24] Diverse and geographically divided peoples can not perceive a common heritage and pursue a common destiny when they have no knowledge, contact, or interaction with one another. Perhaps small, primitive communities can develop with an absence of the mobilization characteristics. However, in a differentiated multi-national state like the Yugoslav, such phenomena as education, exposure, and contact suggest prerequisites that must be present before one can conceive of the development and growth of community.

It is also difficult to conceive of a citizenry with the capacity to rationally and objectively view the complex human relations experienced in a multi-national state if this citizenry interprets these relations from the perspectives of parochialism and traditionalism.[25] And lastly, it is difficult to envision a sense of community among people who do not understand and cooperate with one another. Cooperation and understanding, moreover, are not easy when the populace perceives and acts within the restrictive nature of a particularistic set of values.

It would not only be presumptuous, but most likely false, to suggest that Yugoslavia will soon be characterized by a total sense of community— that its people will have fully learned to communicate, understand, and cooperate with each other. It may not be presumptuous, however, to suggest that the slow but steady influence of further social and economic development may have the effect of aiding this larger process. At the same time, we should not rule out other possible alternatives. That is, such development may have the obverse effect upon inter-ethnic cooperation and so forth. Since the nature of the relationship is an empirical question, it will be treated accordingly in this study. It is clear, however, that social and economic growth is bringing about an increasingly mobilized citizenry, and this mobilization, in essence, means increased communication and cultural contact. The exposed, educated and traveled citizenry is a population trained for the exchange of communicative symbols; a non-mobilized populace, such as certain illiterate sectors of the isolated hinterlands, have lived their entire lives "tuned-in" to an extremely restricted communication network and have associated with perhaps no more than a few hundred people. If the increasing level of mobilization in Yugoslavia is in fact bringing about more modern and less particularistic sets of beliefs, then the presence of community among those formerly isolated sectors may increase. This relationship is a question which of course can be be answered through the survey analysis to follow in subsequent chapters.

The hypothesized evolution of mobilized, modernized, and universalistic characteristics does not necessarily imply that nationalist sentiment, the former issues of "economic nationalism," or demands for increased autonomy, for example, within the society will suddenly subside. They will probably not. But they do suggest that people may begin to approach political questions in a rather different style. Demands may be presented less often in terms of black and white—"all or nothing"—rhetoric. One may expect to find well documented, objective arguments accompanying important requests. Demands and desires presented in this style would seem to reflect the present of at least some minimal level of communication, cooperation, and perhaps understanding, and would appear to be creating a different setting within which the issues of politics are discussed. In short, it is possible to say that under the hypothesized changes, more people would be capable of approaching problems with a capacity to view and interpret them in a manner encouraging negotiation and compromise.[26]

With these thoughts in mind, the study conceptualizes the development of the Yugoslav socialist community in terms of three criteria. The first and lowest order criterion may be thought of as certain levels of communication skills, exposure, and cultural contact on the part of the populace. The second criterion is viewed as a condition of modern, rational values on the part of this same body. And the third is viewed as a set of universalistic norms among the inhabitants of the state on a level that transcends the more narrow boundaries of particularistic concerns. These three criteria can be represented by the social mobilization, modernism, and cultural universalism variables to be utilized in this study. On the basis of this rationale, any community could be ranked along a continuum that represented the degree to which the state had fulfilled these three general conditions (see Figure 3). Higher levels of mobilization, modernism, and universalism suggest a more highly developed community.[27]

FIGURE 3
CONTINUUM BASED UPON THE THREE CRITERIA ASSESSING THE
RELATIVE EXTENT OF COMMUNITY-DEVELOPMENT

Minimal Levels on Three Criteria		Optimal Levels on Three Criteria
Low	DEGREE OF COMMUNITY	High
Mobilization		Mobilization
Modernism		Modernism
Universalism		Universalism

The analysis to follow in the later chapters will focus on Yugoslavia's ability to fulfill the three criteria as defined. The principal hypothesis is that its ability to do so is dependent upon the previously suggested evolutionary relationship of the three variables defined and operationalized for this study.

D. Ordering the Variables

It is necessary to organize the theoretical formulations sketched above for empirical analysis. In that regard, the three individual attributes or variables will be organized as a set of simultaneous equations which may be referred to as a "structural system" of variables.[28] The concern will be with a sub-class of structural systems commonly referred to as "recursive systems" which rules out two-way causation.[29] In effect, after surveying the developmental process in Yugoslavia, the social phenomena incorporated in the mobilization index are viewed as causes of value changes. Although some reciprocal relationship may be evident, it is unlikely that values affect education or mass media exposure to the extent that these characteristics affect values. In this study, then, social mobilization (A) is viewed as positively related to modernism (B) and universalism (C). Modernism (B), in turn, is taken as positively related to universalism (C). The causal chain can be represented simply as:

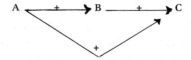

This model of some human elements of the community-building process assumes an evolutionary sequence in the characteristics of an individual. It presupposes a time lag between characteristics, and thus assumes that the largest correlations will occur between the adjacent variables in the causal chain (i.e., r_{AB} and r_{BC}). We would therefore expect the correlation between A and C to be smaller than either the correlation between A and B or B and C.

The following set of equations can be written to represent the relationships between the variables:

1) $A_1 = e_1$ [30]
2) $B_2 = b_{21}A1 + e_2$
3) $C_3 = b_{31}A_1 + b_{32}B_2 + e_3$

A_1 (social mobilization) will be assumed to be an "exogenous" variable, or a variable whose value is determined by factors outside of the recursive system (e_1).[31] B_2 (any value of modernism) is represented by the regression equation in which the mean value of B is traced for each value of A, or in other words, B_2 equals the change (or slope) of 2 on 1 ($B_{21}A_1$) plus the effects of outside variables which will be controlled in the analysis of the data.[32] C_3(any value of universalism) is equal to the change of 3 on 1 ($b_{31}A_1$), plus the change of 3 on 2 ($b_{32}B_2$), and the effects of outside variables which are to be controlled.

Thus, A_1 (social mobilization) is taken to be independent of the other two components. Its value is determined by variables (namely, social and economic development) that are outside the causal system. B_2 (modernism) is dependent upon A_1, and possibly, extraneous variables that are to be controlled. Lastly, C_3 (universalism) is hypothesized as dependent upon both A_1 and B_2, and also possibly, variables outside the system that are to be controlled.

A number of crucial, intervening variables (e_1) are envisaged whose effects upon the system will have to be controlled. One is the variable of ethnicity or nationality. Within the Yugoslav context an individual's nationality is likely to have an intermediate effect between A and B, or any other combination of the components. Take, for example, the Slovenes who may be highly mobilized and quite modern, but somewhat particularistic because of their rather strong cultural tradition and sense of national identity. The reader is only being reminded that the historical experiences of the different national groups in Yugoslavia brought about a diverse mosaic of contrasting national characters. The data may show that some complex of national traits may affect the change dynamics suggested in the model.

Another relevant intervening effect may result from the milieu in which an individual resides. That is, there may be something about the socio-economic environment in which an individual finds himself that influences his propensity for change in accordance with the model. It may be found, for example, that in areas of extreme social and economic deprivation, increases in the levels of social mobilization among a relatively small segment of the population will have little effect in separating them from more traditional and particularistic value sets. The data may indicate that value change among such individuals will be negligible due to the "restraining effect" of the environment surrounding them. Therefore, it will be necessary to apply a number of controls to the data, and in doing so, assess comparatively dynamics of the process by viewing various sub-populations across the country. This "controlling strategy" will prove to be an important part of the analysis. Once the direction and strength of the relationships have been determined within the country-wide population, it will be necessary to examine sub-groups within this larger sample. In this manner it will be possible to see if some of the diversity of land and people found in the South Slavic context have a significant influence upon the change dynamics of the model.

What this means, in effect, is that for research purposes we are conceptualizing the community-building process at the individual level of analysis in terms of a recursive system of variables made up of three causally-linked components. The relationships between the components, however, are expected to be influenced to some determinable extent by variables outside the system, two of the most important of which may be identified as nationality and level of socio-economic development. This system of variables, including the "nationality control," may be illustrated in the following diagram form (see Figure 4).

FIGURE 4
CONCEPTUALIZATION OF A_1, B_2, AND C_3 WITH NATIONALITY CONTROLLED

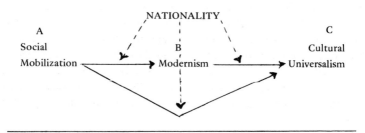

It can be noted in conclusion that the post-war Communist regime hoped to encourage the evolution of a new and different populace by coupling Marxist principles with modernization logic. This study attempts to fit the Yugoslavs' logic to a recursive system of variables. The framework used to organized the logic posited that three components or variables of the individual aspect of community-building are interdependent and of central importance in explaining the overall building process. It was hypothesized that as the prior components in the causal chain varied, the remaining components would also vary according to a determined pattern. All three of these phenomena were discussed and operationalized by using survey data collected from 1186 individuals in Yugoslav society. On the basis of this conceptualization, it was hypothesized that these phenomena will show that the individual with higher education, the individual exposed to wide ranges of information disseminated by the mass media, and the individual widely traveled within and outside of his country (i.e., the mobilized individual), may be expected to assume a different orientation in regard to two contingent value components of the community-building process than does the individual who has an absence or lesser expression of these characteristics. First, it was hypothesized that the individual who possesses these characteristics is more likely to de-emphasize the role of tradition, super-naturalism, fate, familialism, negativism, and irrationalism in defining and understanding the environment surrounding him. Secondly, as a result of the first set of characteristics and also as a result of a "modernized" belief system, it was hypothesized that this individual will tend to be less affected by the usual barriers to further communication, cooperation, and understanding in the Yugoslav context. That is, this individual may be less likely to hold excessive attachments to his own nationality, language, locale, family, and thoughts—namely, those attachments most likely to restrict the evolution of a higher form of Yugoslav identity.

What significance, one might ask, does this conceptualization have to a theory of community-building? The question might best be answered by quoting one widely accepted finding among scholars of the modernization process. Harbison and Myers, among others, have contended that "education is the key that unlocks the door to modernization."[33] The data to be presented in the remaining chapters suggest that there is good reason and solid empirical justification for this finding, but perhaps more importantly, that it should be broadened to include a number of other distinct, though closely related, phenomena. Of course, education aids in this process, but when coupling the idea of modernization with community-building in the Yugoslav context, we may find that it is also of major importance that this individual be listening, viewing, reading, traveling, and in general, exposing himself to the rich diversity that exists within the country. This behavior and the resultant value systems may never solve the "nationality problem" or other domestic concerns of immediate importance to Yugoslavia, but it may well be that it has already significantly encouraged the communication, cooperation, and understanding needed to approach the problems. This in itself may be a supreme accomplishment within an internally complex society such as Yugoslavia.

CHAPTER IV

SOCIAL MOBILIZATION AND CHANGING VALUE SYSTEMS: COUNTRY-WIDE OBSERVATIONS

A. *Introduction*

Although the preceding chapters discussed some of the historical forces acting upon the Yugoslav citizen, as well as a number of socio-economic contours defining his milieu, little information has been offered concerning the personal characteristics of the 1186 individuals included in this study's country-wide survey sample. This chapter will provide this information by addressing itself to two central objectives. First, it will characterize the Yugoslav individual found in the sample by viewing some of his social characteristics and personal values, as well as some of the relationships that exist between these two sets of individual attributes. Secondly, by using these attributes to form the three central variables discussed in the previous chapter, it will consider the applicability and explanatory power of the three variables in terms of the model outlined above.

The first objective requires a close analysis of the 1186 individuals included in the country-wide sample. But before viewing the sample in terms of the individual attributes comprising the three basic variables, it may be instructive to remind the reader of some of the definitional qualities of these variables. The first of the two variables composed of value orientations was called modernism. Although there are, of course, no single definitions of the traditional or modern man that all social scientists accept and use, there are some areas of agreement as to the nature of the qualities that distinguish between these two ideal types. At the same time, it should be noted that the specific qualities that are distinguishing in one society or social setting may be inapplicable in another. No one would deny that the particular qualities that differentiate traditional and modern men in Yugoslavia as compared to Mexico may be rather different. Therefore, it is important that the conception to be used in this study shares commonalities with other societies, but at the same time, allows for qualities that have particular application in the Yugoslav context. In order to accomplish this, traditionalism was defined as an inter-related system of values that defines events and behavior within Yugoslav society on the basis of "irrational and negativist" norms.[1] Modernism, or the values of modern man, in contrast, represents an inter-related set of values that denies the importance of these norms. This allows the selection of specific values that have particular application in the Yugoslav setting, while still maintaining some similarity to the nature of the same qualities in other countries.[2]

The second variable composed of value orientations was called cultural universalism-particularism. This variable, or more specifically, the belief system of the universalistic man, was defined as an inter-related complex of values that tended to engender further communication, cooperation, and understanding among different social sectors within the diverse Yugoslav context. The specific orientations in this larger value system represent the extent of an individual's attachment and loyalty to more provincial or parochial objects within the Yugoslav setting. This complex of values, therefore, permits an investigator to distinguish between the characteristics of the particularistic and universalistic person. Accordingly, the particularistic person is one who stresses the importance of such elements while the "non-particularist" denies their importance.

These two sets of values (i.e., modernism and universalism) were viewed as dependent upon a certain set of social and demographic attributes of the individual. In a fashion similar to that of Inkeles, it was hypothesized that a set of "mobilizing forces" was likely to bring about changes in these two systems of values.[3] First, it was hypothesized that certain attributes of the individual (e.g., increased education) tend to bring about a value system that diminishes the importance of "irrational and negativist" norms. Then, it was hypothesized that this set of values, along with the noted mobilizing attributes, were likely to decrease one's attachment to particularistic elements. But before making a thorough analysis of these relationships, it will be instructive to take a closer look at the mobilizing characteristics within the country-wide sample.

B. Characteristics of Mobilization

A clearer picture of the Yugoslav individual can be gained by considering his mobilizing characteristics. When viewing the sample in this respect, the data show that most respondents have attained some level of education—in fact, only three per cent are illiterate or without any formal education. Thirty-two per cent have received some schooling in the elementary grades, while a large majority (65 per cent) have attained some level beyond elementary school. When considering exposure to mass media, the data indicate that almost half of the sample (510 individuals) are characterized by extremely low levels of daily usage. Among this section of the sample, daily exposure to radio, television, and the press is extremely low (see Table 1). However, the twenty-seven per cent characterized by "medium" levels of exposure, as well as the thirty per cent classified as "high," show progressively higher levels of usage in each of the three media. Diversity in the sample is also found in terms of internal and external travel. Thirteen per cent of the sample were never outside of the culture-

TABLE 1

RADIO, TELEVISION, AND NEWSPAPER UTILIZATION
BY EXPOSURE LEVEL

	PERCENT WHO DAILY . . .			
MASS MEDIA				
EXPOSURE	Listen to	Watch	Read	
	Radio	Television	Newspaper	N
Low	37	16	14	510
Medium	64	53	44	320
High	79	74	68	356
TOTAL	61	47	39	1186

region in which they were born.[4] This sector of Yugoslav society represents a very immobile and parochial population. Individuals in this sector are likely to communicate primarily with members of their own village, and thus with people of similar ethnic and religious backgrounds.[5] Illustrative of this physical isolation is the fact that the Slovene from northern Yugoslavia is likely to be almost as strange to the peasant of the isolated village of Nevesinje[6] as might be a foreign student from Africa.

On the other hand, some sectors of the sample have traveled rather widely. Twenty-one per cent have been to at least three culture-regions in addition to the one in which they were born; forty per cent have traveled to four, five, or six; and, twenty-six per cent of the sample have traveled to seven or more. The percentage breakdown represents a range from people who have made little attempt or had no opportunity to travel at all to a sizable portion who have been in all ten regions of the country, a feat which is particularly impressive when taking into consideration the difficulties of transportation that have marked the country in the past.

In terms of travel outside of Yugoslavia, a sizable portion of the sample has been abroad. In fact, forty-one per cent have been outside of the country one or more times, while the remaining sector of the population has not journeyed beyond Yugoslav borders. It is worthwhile noting that a predominance of this external travel is by inhabitants of the two northern republics, Slovenia and Croatia. It is widely recognized that when the inhabitants of these two more developed regions travel, they go north to Italy,

Austria, and Germany, and seldom south (although Croatians often go south-west to Dalmatia), while the inhabitants of the south often visit the north and Dalmatia but very seldom get outside of the country.[7] Therefore, while the northern populations are "high" on external travel and "low" on internal movement, the more southern populations represent the opposite characteristics.[8]

Overall, the data suggest the presence of a population in Yugoslavia that runs the entire gamut from the highly educated, highly exposed and traveled sector to those individuals who can not read, who seldom listen to the radio, watch television, or read newspapers, and who never travel far from home. These contrasting types suggest the basis for differentiating value expression.

C. Value Characteristics

Perhaps the best way to examine the value characteristics of the sample would be to relate them to the mobilizing attributes just mentioned. That is, now that we have some idea of the educational structure of the sample, mobility patterns, and so forth, a consideration of their meaning in terms of a number of values comprising the Modernism scale should be instructive. A simple cross-tabulation can show whether one's education, as suggested by Inkeles and others, is related to more modern beliefs.[9] Consider, for example, the responses to one of the most basic indicators distinguishing between the "traditional" and the "modern" man in Yugoslavia, that is, the role of "the supernatural in one's life" (see Table 2). The percentage breakdown in the table shows convincingly that as the Yugoslav becomes more highly educated, he in turn becomes more skeptical of the role of supernatural forces in determining the course of events. Whereas over half of those people with no education agree that "the world is governed by supernatural forces," only a very small minority of the most highly educated do so. Overall, the table convincingly demonstrates the cumulative effect of increased education. With each added level of education, the data indicate a greater percentage of the group disagreeing with the influence of supernatural forces.

The nature of traditional life has emphasized and re-emphasized that man's fate is ordained by Allah (or other appropriate supernatural forces) and, in doing so, has underlined man's inability to determine his own future. An Orthodox peasant living in one of the most isolated regions of Serbia once told me, "What am I, as one individual, against the forces of the almighty? My ancestors saw the coming and ravaging of the Turk. They had no control over their destiny then, just as I have none today." And after the major destruction of a Bosnian city (Banja Luka) by the November, 1969, earthquake, the same remark was heard time and time

TABLE 2

IMPORTANCE OF THE ROLE OF SUPERNATURAL FORCES
BY EDUCATION

THE WORLD IS GOVERNED BY SUPERNATURAL FORCES
WHICH PREDETERMINE THE COURSE OF EVENTS . . .

(percentages)

EDUCATION	Strongly Agree	Agree	Disagree	Strongly Disagree	N
none	31	25	25	19	32
0-4 years	22	25	29	24	236
4-8 years	14	16	29	41	140
Completed Vocational School	8	13	29	50	163
Completed Gymnasium	6	8	12	74	228
Attended College	5	6	13	76	365
Total	11	12	21	56	1164

Gamma = .481   Sig. $>$.001

again through television and newspaper reports. "What has 'he' brought us now? Just as we were beginning to build and develop our land and city, we see it crumbled at our feet. And we must stand helplessly and watch; we have no control of our own destiny."

The differences between "moderns" and "traditionals" became increasingly clear in the aftermath of this tragic earthquake in the northern section of Bosnia-Hercegovina. While the city planners and engineers were making progressive, new plans for building one of the most modern cities of Yugoslavia, the recent peasant immigrants of Banja Luka were talking of going back to the land where the destruction was not so great and the life less complicated. Interestingly, a completely different perspective on the destruction resulted. The "moderns" saw it as an opportunity for man to exhibit control of his environment by planning and constructing new buildings that the land had never seen before. By way of contrast, the destruction represented another chapter in the role of "pre-determined and uncontrollable events" in the eyes of the "traditionals."[10]

Consideration will now be directed toward the effects of the other three indicators in the mobilization variable. It will be instructive to note whether they also suggest some influence in bringing about the more modern position on this particular belief. An examination of the figures presented in the cross-tabulations on the following pages indicates that all suggest a similar modernizing influence (see Tables 3, 4, and 5).[11] In effect, the figures indicate that as exposure to the media—as well as internal and external travel levels—increases, so does the tendency to disagree with the importance of supernatural forces in controlling events.

These findings parallel what is already known about the traditional man in the country. Basically, he is an individual who has remained apart or isolated from the changes that are taking place around him. He is likely to be without a television set (approximately two-thirds of all Yugoslav families are) and seldom listens to the radio.[12] What he can gain from the newspapers is restricted because of his limited reading ability. Furthermore, it is seldom that he leaves the surroundings of his own village, not to mention the absence of travel to the far-reaches of his own country, or to destinations outside of Yugoslavia. In short, the figures in the tables given below suggest that this general isolation from communication stimuli is closely related to an emphasis on the supernatural and an acceptance of one's fate. However, the individual possessing the contrasting value orientation, and incidentally a sector of Yugoslavia that is inevitably growing as social and economic development continues, is a sector that has not remained apart from the surrounding stimuli. This sector represents the readers, viewers, listeners, and travelers. Within its ranks are likely to be the university student, the young politician, and the urban planner rebuilding the city of Banja Luka; furthermore, these individuals are likely to be working in rather different environments from that of their fathers'. For example, consider the planner in Banja Luka and what took place in the aftermath of the earthquake. He was probably called from an institute in Sarajevo, Ljubljana, Zagreb, Belgrade, or another major city. Now he finds himself attacking new problems, establishing new friendships, and forming new working relationships that may alter his entire life. This individual, and many more like him, may have the effect of changing the social and political environment of the country over the coming years in a fashion to be described at length in later sections of this study.

TABLE 3

IMPORTANCE OF THE ROLE OF SUPERNATURAL FORCES
BY MASS MEDIA EXPOSURE

THE WORLD IS GOVERNED BY SUPERNATURAL FORCES
WHICH PREDETERMINE THE COURSE OF EVENTS . . .
(*percentages*)

MASS MEDIA EXPOSURE	Strongly Agree	Agree	Disagree	Strongly Disagree	N
Low	16	20	28	36	496
Medium	11	10	18	61	318
High	2	4	13	81	348
Total	11	12	21	56	1162*

* The sample will not always reflect the total 1186 respondents since "no answers" have been dropped from the tables.

Gamma = .518 Sig. > .001

TABLE 4

IMPORTANCE OF THE ROLE OF SUPERNATURAL FORCES
BY INTERNAL TRAVEL

THE WORLD IS GOVERNED BY SUPERNATURAL FORCES
WHICH PREDETERMINE THE COURSE OF EVENTS . . .
(*percentages*)

INTERNAL TRAVEL	Strongly Agree	Agree	Disagree	Strongly Disagree	N
Very Low	26	23	29	22	156
Low	13	20	31	36	248
High	7	8	18	67	464
Very High	6	8	13	73	296
Total	11	12	21	56	1164

Gamma = .450 Sig. > .001

TABLE 5

IMPORTANCE OF THE ROLE OF SUPERNATURAL FORCES
BY EXTERNAL TRAVEL

	THE WORLD IS GOVERNED BY SUPERNATURAL FORCES WHICH PREDETERMINE THE COURSE OF EVENTS ... *(percentages)*				
EXTERNAL TRAVEL	Strongly Agree	Agree	Disagree	Strongly Disagree	N
Low	12	15	24	49	685
High	9	8	16	57	476
Total	11	12	21	56	1161

Gamma = .285 Sig. > .01

The value set of the "modern man" is represented of course by more than one dimension. Consideration will now be directed toward another aspect of this belief system, one that is also an important differentiator between the "traditional" and the "modern" in the country. This aspect concerns the relationship between parent and child and has particular relevance in Yugoslavia because of the solid, patriarchal family-structure throughout its history.[13] Erlich has suggested that with the increased development of the economy (e.g., money exchange) and society (e.g., dissolution of the *zadruga*), the structure of the family and authority of the parent has tended to change. She notes that generally the structure of the family has tended to become less differentiated (i.e., less hierarchial) and the authority of the parent has tended to weaken.[14] However, even today in the less developed sectors, the importance of and emphasis on parental authority and childhood obedience is often clear, and is particularly characteristic of the more traditional men in the village.[15] Now let us consider how the 1186 respondents felt about this question, and also how their responses were affected by the mobilization items.

The most apparent finding when viewing the figures presented in the cross tabulation is the overall percentage of Yugoslavs who "strongly agree" with the dominant importance of childhood obedience (see Table 6).

TABLE 6

IMPORTANCE OF PARENTAL AUTHORITY BY EDUCATION

EDUCATION	THE MOST IMPORTANT THING FOR CHILDREN IS THAT THEY LEARN TO OBEY THEIR PARENTS ...				
	Strongly Agree	(percentages) Agree	Disagree	Strongly Disagree	N
None	91	9	0	0	35
0-4 years	68	21	10	1	244
4-8 years	48	27	20	5	143
Completed Vocational School	51	28	13	8	167
Completed Gymnasium	26	30	32	12	229
Attended College	23	27	38	12	368
Total	42	26	24	8	1184

Gamma = .443   Sig. >.001

When considering the entire sample, 42 per cent "strongly agree" with this statement and another 26 per cent "agree." Therefore, well over half of the sample place a considerable amount of importance on this norm when viewing and interpreting events and behavior in their society. The second point of interest in this table is the clear linear relationship between education and levels of agreement with the value premise. The modernizing influence of education is again suggested with successively higher levels of education showing cumulatively higher levels of disagreement with this value. The most un-educated and most educated groups show sharp differences in their acceptance of the value. Illustrative is the fact that of those with no formal education, 91 per cent "strongly agree" and all "agree" to some extent, whereas only 23 per cent of the most highly educated sector "strongly agree."

An interesting aspect of this phenomenon can be clearly viewed within the more highly educated centers of the country today. While sizable sectors of the student populations in the larger cities are dancing nightly at the local "discothèques" until one or two o'clock in the morning, such behavior and hours remain unheard of in the villages.[16] This is not only a result of education, of course, but a part of the larger character and value set that is being described in this section.

When looking at the exposure to mass media and travel variables, rather

TABLE 7

IMPORTANCE OF PARENTAL AUTHORITY BY MASS
MEDIA EXPOSURE

THE MOST IMPORTANT THING FOR CHILDREN IS
THAT THEY LEARN TO OBEY THEIR PARENTS . . .

MASS MEDIA EXPOSURE	Strongly Agree	(percentages) Agree	Disagree	Strongly Disagree	N
Low	61	23	13	3	509
Medium	35	30	26	9	324
High	19	27	39	15	349
Total	42	26	24	8	1182

Gamma = .497 Sig. > .001

TABLE 8

IMPORTANCE OF PARENTAL AUTHORITY
BY INTERNAL TRAVEL

THE MOST IMPORTANT THING FOR CHILDREN IS
THAT THEY LEARN TO OBEY THEIR PARENTS . . .

INTERNAL TRAVEL	Strongly Agree	(percentages) Agree	Disagree	Strongly Disagree	N
Very Low	68	24	6	2	165
Low	50	27	19	4	249
High	34	27	29	10	471
Very High	30	25	32	12	299
Total	42	26	24	8	1184

Gamma = .497 Sig. > .001

similar results are found (see Tables 7 and 8). Representative of the find-ings is the following example: while 61 per cent of the persons with low exposure to the mass media strongly maintain that the most important thing for children to learn is parental obedience, only 19 per cent of the "highly exposed" feel similarly. Furthermore, other attitudinal indicators making up the Modernism scale reflect similar (almost identical) pat-terns. In fact, all indicators used to construct the Mobilization index correlated *highly* and *significantly* with the items comprising the Modern-ism scale.

After having viewed a number of items making up the Mobilization and Modernism scales, two main points should be clear. The first concerns the heterogeneity of the population. There were notable ranges in educa-tion, exposure to the instruments of mass media, and travel, as well as a wide dispersion of responses on all of the relevant value orientations. The heterogeneous posture becomes even more meaningful when the nature of social and economic change is considered, as well as the argument that was made earlier concerning its dynamics. That is, the process of social devel-opment does not move across and throughout the entire society in an equal and even "wave." If it did, we could expect more homogeneity in the sample. However, as it is, increases in education are reaching primarily the younger segments of the society. Education has become widespread only within the last twenty years of the country's history and those over forty-five years were and are unlikely to be greatly affected by this form of social change. It should be noted, however, that there is a vigorous attempt being made to reach this population through the "Peoples" and "Workers" universities. Nevertheless, many of the changes in social life experienced by the country are "missing" segments of the population and this is clearly shown in the data.

One aspect of this "uneven process of change" results in the often used comparisons between city and village. There is nothing inherent in the character of the peasant residing in the village that makes him less likely to change, or to change at a slower rate. However, there is something about the realities of social and economic life that explains the presence of these contrasts. Namely, and as is well known, the dynamics of modern industri-alizing economies create an inevitable process of faster and greater devel-opment in the cities. Industrialization is greater there; people move to the cities to accept new jobs in the factories, and as a result, often earn larger incomes. This sets off a dynamic at both the individual and societal levels, and the larger process of social development is in motion. The person in the village immediately finds himself at a disadvantage. Illustrative is the fact that because of the lack of resources in these more isolated areas, the schools of the village have traditionally been inferior to those in Belgrade or other major cities in the more developed areas. Furthermore, the whole syndrome of attitudes and incentives favoring increased and higher education is likely to be higher in the cities.

Communication media are also more prevalent in the cities, as well as the resources and abilities to travel.[17] The availability of other institutions of information dissemination explains another aspect of the "gap" between   city and village in Yugoslavia. While newspapers, libraries, universities, public lectures, theaters, galleries and other similar institutions are widespread in Belgrade, they are often absent when traveling one hundred miles into isolated areas.[18] In short, the differentiation found in environment and value systems is an inevitable and perhaps unavoidable result of the change process in Yugoslavia.[19]

However, it is also necessary to note and account for the fact that while an individual may be "reached" by one modernizing influence (e.g., travel), he may be missed by another (e.g., education). A current example could be represented by a member of Yugoslavia's large population working abroad. That is, while a Macedonian may have traveled through the entire length of the country and also through Austria to accept a job in West Germany, he may still be relatively "unmobilized" even after having traveled and worked abroad for a few years due to his low level of education or even an inability to read. Other examples (high education, low mass media exposure, and low internal and external travel) are also commonplace in other situations. The method of summated indexing described earlier and to be used in this study accounts for such differences by taking into consideration, not only the individual's relative degree of mobilization on one indicator, but also the relative degrees on all four indicators simultaneously.

The second consideration that is readily apparent after a review of the mobilization and traditionalism variables is the high degree of interrelationship between their component parts. A consideration of the overall correlation matrix shows that knowledge of an individual's ranking on a mobilization item (e.g., education) permits one to predict with considerable accuracy his ranking on any modernism-traditionalism item (see Table 9). The data indicate, for example, with respect to the .50 *gamma* coefficient between exposure to the mass media and "parental authority," that there is 50 per cent more agreement than disagreement in the ordering of the two scales. In other words, as education increases, de-emphasis on "parental authority" tends to increase at a substantial rate. Overall, the correlation matrix illustrates empirically the relationships that were hypothesized earlier in more theoretical terms. It would seem that attention must indeed be paid to the idea of the "modernizing influences" found in the mobilization items.

TABLE 9

CORRELATION MATRIX: ITEMS COMPRISING THE SOCIAL
MOBILIZATION INDEX AND MODERNISM SCALE

SOCIAL MOBILIZATION ITEMS	VALUES COMPRISING MODERNISM SCALE[a]				
	A	B	C	D	E
Education	.36	.44	.28	.48	.27
Mass Media Exposure . . .	.42	.50	.30	.52	.26
Internal Travel	.26	.33	.14	.45	.29
External Travel	.16	.41	.25	.29	.26

[a] Responses to the values were originally coded in terms of a four-point, agree-disagree Likert-type scale. The capital letters in the table refer to the following value propositions: A) If you don't keep all four eyes open, people will exploit and deceive you; B) The most important thing for children is that they learn to obey their parents; C) In order to fulfill their personal goals and personal desires individuals must compete and subdue one another; D) The world is governed by supernatural forces which predetermine the course of events; E) The children of great parents are endowed with the qualities of their parents.

Now we can move on to a consideration of the effects of the mobilization items on values of universalism within the Yugoslav context. Upon examining the matrix resulting from an inter-correlation of the items in the two variables, the crucial dynamics of the change process become clear (see Table 10). That is, the presence of a positive relationship was hypothesized earlier between mobilization and modernism. Upon an examination of the data in the last section, the data supported the hypothesis. It was also hypothesized in the previous chapter that although a relationship might exist between mobilization and universalism, it would not be particularly strong without the prior and mediatory influence of the modernism variable. That is, the discussion noted that the mobilized person is not always non-particularistic, but suggested that he is more likely to be when he also holds modern values. Social mobilization, it was maintained, affects universalism through its effect on modern values. The three hypothesized linkages are shown in diagram form along with the suggested strengths of relationship (see Figure 5). The correlation coefficients registered in

TABLE 10

CORRELATION MATRIX: ITEMS COMPRISING THE SOCIAL
MOBILIZATION INDEX AND CULTURAL UNIVERSALISM SCALE

SOCIAL MOBILIZATION ITEMS	VALUES COMPRISING CULTURAL UNIVERSALISM SCALE[a]				
	F	G	H	I	J
Education	.19	.34	.23	.23	.49
Mass Media Exposure	.17	.40	.24	.21	.49
Internal Travel	–[b]	.19	.25	.21	.29
External Travel	.17	.34	––	––	.37

[a]The capital letters refer to the following value propositions: F) It is important to know the history of your family; G) It is important for a man to speak his own dialect; H) Nationality is important in our country; I) It is better that a judge whom you know pass judgment on you, for example from your own locale, than to be judged by someone you don't know; J) It is not necessary to speak with individuals whose thoughts are in opposition to ours.

[b]Significance at the .05 level was not attained in the empty cells.

FIGURE 5

THREE VARIABLE MODEL WITH SUGGESTED STRENGTHS
OF RELATIONSHIP

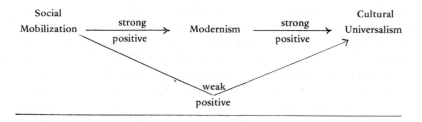

Tables 9 and 10 add support to these hypothesized relationships. While the coefficients in the mobilization-modernism matrix were all significant and of considerable strength, the mobilization-universalism matrix exhibits generally weaker relationships where significance was not attained.

When moving on to a consideration of the relationship between modernism and universalism, these suggestions receive further empirical support (see Table 11). The data not only indicate that every possible relationship is positively correlated at a significant level, but also illustrate that the size of the coefficients are considerably higher than those present in the

TABLE 11

CORRELATION MATRIX: ITEMS COMPRISING THE MODERNISM
AND CULTURAL UNIVERSALISM SCALES

VALUES COMPRISING MODERNISM SCALE	VALUES COMPRISING CULTURAL UNIVERSALISM SCALE				
	F	G	H	I	J
A	19	.31	.28	.24	.33
B	29	.42	.28	.23	.49
C	23	.31	.22	.23	.33
D	25	.36	.34	.32	.50
E	17	.30	.28	.29	.36

former mobilization-modernism matrix. When devoting individual attention to a number of the relationships, the phenomenon takes on both complexity and greater clarity. For example, one important indicator of the "particularistic man" in Yugoslavia revolves around the idea of language. The language that one speaks, the dialect that one chooses to use, and also one's feelings about the importance of using it, tell a great deal about a person in Yugoslavia.[20] Earlier it was suggested that orientations such as these would tend to depend upon one's posture on the modernism items, but does an examination of the data also give support to this contention?

When viewing the relationship between the earlier mentioned "importance of parental authority" and the "importance of speaking one's own dialect," a strong positive correlation is shown (see Table 12). This finding suggests that if an individual places importance upon childhood obedience and parental authority he is also likely to emphasize the importance of speaking one's own local dialect. In other words, if an individual takes a traditionalistic stance on the first value premise, he is likely to assume a particularistic posture on the second.

It is also interesting to consider the overall posture found in the sample on the question of language. The data indicate that fifty per cent of the respondents take an extremely dogmatic posture on the question by emphatically agreeing (i.e., "strongly agree") with the importance of the

TABLE 12

IMPORTANCE OF ONE'S OWN DIALECT BY IMPORTANCE
OF PARENTAL AUTHORITY

IMPORTANCE OF PARENTAL AUTHORITY . . .	IT IS IMPORTANT FOR A MAN TO SPEAK HIS OWN DIALECT . . .				
	Strongly Agree	(*percentages*) Agree	Disagree	Strongly Disagree	N
Strongly Agree	68	12	10	10	462
Agree	46	27	17	10	292
Disagree	32	20	27	21	278
Strongly Disagree	26	12	26	36	95
Total	50	18	17	15	1127

Gamma = .416   Sig.>.001

idea. Other items in the Universalism-Particularism variable demonstrate similar tendencies. In this regard, the data show that 56 per cent agree to the "importance of the nationality factor within the Yugoslav context." Furthermore, when speaking about the importance of one's own value system, or the legal treatment that one receives in his own locale, it becomes evident that the degree of particularism depends upon the given question. For example, 68 per cent of the sample feel that they can receive as fair a trial in another area in Yugoslavia, or from a jury and judge that they do not know, as from friends in their own locale. However, the remaining 22 per cent reflect a strong form of particularism that clearly attaches value in regard to their legal, political, or administrative success or failure to friends within their own community. The survey data also show a small but significant minority who are unwilling to "step outside" from their own system of values. In this regard, 21 per cent of the sample contends that it is unimportant and unnecessary to communicate with individuals who represent different beliefs and values. This minority within the sample reflects a value orientation which is certainly not conducive to the communication, cooperation, and understanding likely to engender the further development of the Yugoslav socialist community.

Again it is necessary to consider some of the dynamics that engender value systems which exhibit the contrasting orientation, that is, a willingness to communicate with opposing elements within the diverse Yugoslav context. Namely, are aspects of the modern value set likely to encourage this openness toward and tolerance of opposing groups, individuals, and ideas as earlier formulations suggested? The coefficients produced when correlating indicators of modernism with this particular value suggested that such is the case (see Table 11). In fact, the data indicated that all items purporting to differentiate between the "traditional" and "modern" are significantly related to this orientation. By cross-tabulating one of these items with the "willingness to communicate" value, a better idea of the relationship can be gained (see Table 13). The data indicate that these 635 individuals who earlier strongly disagreed with the importance of the supernatural, now predominantly· (73 per cent) show a characteristic of universalism by emphasizing the need to communicate with opposing individuals. The figures and the *gamma* shown in Table 13 are only

---

- TABLE 13

WILLINGNESS TO COMMUNICATE BY BELIEF
IN SUPERNATURAL FORCES

"WORLD IS   IT IS NOT NECESSARY TO SPEAK WITH
GOVERNED BY   INDIVIDUALS WHOSE THOUGHTS ARE
SUPERNATURAL   IN OPPOSITION TO OURS . . .
FORCES . . ."

	Strongly Agree	(*percentages*) Agree	Disagree	Strongly Disagree	N
Strongly Agree	36	7	23	34	125
Agree	21	18	34	27	142
Disagree	15	8	37	40	241
Strongly Disagree	9	3	15	73	653
Total	15	6	23	56	1161

Gamma = .502 Sig. > .001

---

representative of the other twenty-four value relationship registered in Table 11. The twenty-four coefficients listed in that matrix indicate that if an individual possesses modern values, he is likely to hold a universalistic set of orientations. Without exception, the coefficients lend empirical support to the diagram listed in Figure 5.

The data described above characterized the sample as a heterogeneous population representing diverse social attributes and contrasting value systems. The preceding analysis addressed itself to the question of whether any patterns existed in this diversity, or whether the individual characteristics were "jumbled" in an indiscriminate manner. By correlating the attributes and values, the data showed that some patterns existed, and further, that they suggested the linkages of the model outlined in Chapter Three. First, the inter-correlations identified the positive relationships between the forces of social mobilization and the values of the "modern man." Then, the coefficients delineated the relationships (although as suggested earlier, of a considerably weaker nature) between the mobilization forces and values of universalism. This weaker linkage suggested the intermediating role of the modernism factor as was also outlined in Chapter Three. Then, when considering the values of modernism in greater detail, the data showed that they correlated highly with items in the Universalism scale, and in so doing, reinforced the positive association between the indicators of social mobilization and the values of universalism.

D. Application of the Model

It is now possible to simplify the hypothesized linkages in the model by reducing the fourteen individual characteristics to the three central variables. While the foregoing section considered the entire grouping of indicators in order to provide a more detailed picture of the individual, this section will limit itself to the three basic variables. This strategy will permit consideration of the model in the clearest and most parsimonious manner.

The model hypothesized an evolutionary sequence in the developing characteristics of an individual. An evolutionist conceptualization of this type presupposes, of course, a time lag between the individual characteristics used to operationalize the three variables. If the conceptualization is accurate, correlations between adjacent variables will be larger than the correlations between variables separated in the "causal" chain. Accordingly, the mobilization-modernism (A-B) and modernism-universalism (B-C) associations should be stronger than the mobilization-universalism (A-C).

When viewing the model and the coefficients summarizing the relationships, the appropriateness and utility of the conceptualization is shown (see Figure 6). The model exhibits that the envelopment of a large number of characteristics into a smaller number of fundamental variables identifies a basic and crucial dynamic in value change among individuals in Yugoslavia today. First, let us direct attention toward the initial variable since the formulation in the previous chapter, as well as those of other scholars, suggested that the forces of mobilization possess changing qualities. The *gamma* coefficients registered in the model suggest that the variable does in fact set off a change dynamic that engenders more modern and less particularistic value sets among members of this sample of 1186 interviewees selected from throughout the country. This relationship raises

FIGURE 6

THREE VARIABLE MODEL: COUNTRY-WIDE SAMPLE

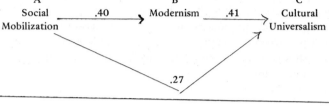

crucial implications for future value change in the society since it is known that the mobilization stimuli will continue to proliferate with further social and economic development.

Previous sections in the study also showed that a cumulative impact was to be exerted by the mobilization characteristics. These sections suggested that, by bracketing together a number of specific processes of change within an individual's societal experience, an overall attribute of the individual was derived that possesses changing qualities. A brief consideration of the cross-tabulation of mobilization and modernism verifies the cumulative effect of the variable (see Table 14). With each successive increase in the level of mobilization, increases in the level of modernism are indicated. In the extreme lower right-hand corner, the most mobilized, modern individuals are found; that is, individuals in this cell reflect the most mobilized characteristics as well as the most modernized values in the sample.

The next link in the chain (i.e., B-C) is of similar importance to the model. It was suggested that the mobilized, modern man would also tend to be less particularistic. The data show that the hypothesis is again verified; that is, the greater the level of modernism, the greater the level of universalism. A consideration of the percentages presented in a cross-tabulation of the two scales illustrates that if an individual ranks high on one scale, he seldom ranks low on the other (see Table 15). In fact, the upper right and lower left cells in the cross-tabulation are found without individuals. The zero registered in the lower left cell indicates that within the total sample, no individuals reflect the highest level of modern values, and at the same time, the lowest level of universalism. Furthermore, the upper right cell indicates the obverse—namely, the most traditional respondents in the sample are never the most universalistic. The clustering of individuals in the lower right cells represent the ideal type under analysis in this study. They represent the sector of the society which is most highly educated,

TABLE 14

LEVEL OF MODERNISM BY LEVEL OF MOBILIZATION

LEVEL OF MOBILIZATION[a]	LEVEL OF MODERNISM						
	Low		(percentages)			High	
	1	2	3	4	5	6	N
Low							
1	23	13	33	27	2	2	103
2	13	17	34	29	2	5	142
3	9	10	41	32	3	5	111
4	9	15	37	32	5	2	167
5	7	8	31	26	13	15	108
6	3	8	33	28	6	22	150
7	1	3	27	29	21	19	117
8	0	3	24	27	19	27	142
9	0	4	28	17	16	35	107
High							
Total	7	9	32	28	9	14	1147

Gamma = .400   Sig. > .001

TABLE 15

LEVEL OF CULTURAL UNIVERSALISM BY LEVEL OF MODERNISM

LEVEL OF MODERNISM	LEVEL OF CULTURAL UNIVERSALISM						
	Low		(percentages)			High	
	1	2	3	4	5	6	N
Low							
1	35	23	31	7	4	0	77
2	14	15	46	17	8	0	94
3	12	14	31	27	12	4	344
4	6	12	33	29	14	6	303
5	2	7	31	20	24	16	104
6	0	4	27	20	37	12	157
High							
Total	9	12	32	23	17	7	1079

Gamma = .410   Sig.>.001

most exposed to the mass media, and most traveled within and outside of the country. They are a people who are reading, communicating, and traveling and their postures on the Modernism and Universalism scales show that they view and interpret events within their society and the world on the bases of modern and non-particularistic norms.

It is necessary to apply some controls to the model at this point. For example, it is important to know if the modernism variable is related to universalism irrespective of levels of mobilization. This picture of the relationship between the two attributes can be attained when those populations with high and low levels of mobilization are viewed separately (see Figure 7). When so doing, we find that among both the "mobilized" and "non-mobilized" the same significant relationship continues to exist.[21] This means that "causal" significance can be attached to the modernism

---

FIGURE 7

THREE VARIABLE MODEL WITH MOBILIZATION CONTROLLED

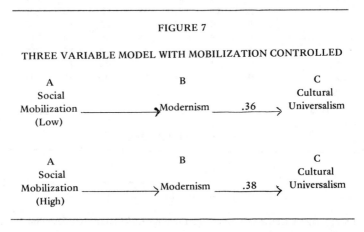

---

variable regardless of the presence or absence of mobilization. However, since it was shown that mobilized persons are much more inclined to reflect modern value sets, the mobilization variable continues to represent the crucial variable in the chain.

The third possible linkage within the model represents the effect of the forces of mobilization on universalistic values. Although the data identify a significant *gamma* correlation of .27, it is considerably weaker than those representing the other linkages (see Figure 6). Hence, although increased mobilization tends to bring about a more tolerant and open value set, the "causal" capability appears to be rather limited. While mobilization was seen to exert a strong influence in bringing about the values of the "modern man," now it exhibits a rather weak affect on the values of universalism. This fits with earlier formulations which hypothesized a time lag between the changing values of the individual. Therefore, since it was hypothesized that modernized values are likely to precede non-particularistic values, the pathway which passes through the modernism variable (i.e., A→B→C) will exhibit a stronger coefficient than the pathway (i.e., A→C) which circumvents the causally prior set of values. Clearly then, the "chain" must go through the mediating modernism variable, for the data indicate that it is only after a "mobilized man" holds a modern value set that he is also most likely to become universalistic.

Again, however, it is necessary to apply a control to the model. It is important to ascertain whether the strength of this "mobilization-universalism" relationship changes when holding modernism constant. Hypothetically, there may be a stronger relationship between the two variables once the intervening effect of modernism has been stabilized. However, even after applying this control, the data show the same relationship between A and C (see Figure 8). Therefore, the effect of mobilization upon universalism for both "moderns" and "traditionals" remains negligible. In the first, the *gamma* coefficient of .16 attains significance only at the .10 level, and the second coefficient of .26 (although significant at the .01 level) is of rather limited strength. The data have shown that the dominant and statistically most powerful pattern is to become mobilized, modern, and then, universalistic.[22]

The evolution of individual attributes just charted has crucial implications to the process of community-building. First, Yugoslav planners forecast that further social and economic development will bring about an even more highly mobilized citizenry in the future. More people are acquiring higher levels of education, and considerably larger numbers of people

FIGURE 8

THREE VARIABLE MODEL WITH MODERNISM CONTROLLED

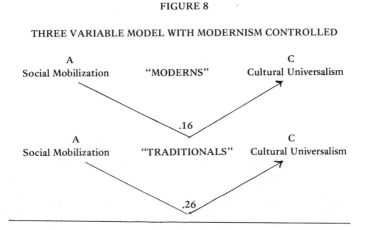

A
Social Mobilization   "MODERNS"   Cultural Universalism

.16

A
Social Mobilization   "TRADITIONALS"   Cultural Universalism

.26

are "tuning in" to the instruments of mass media. In addition, better transportation facilities and a more affluent citizenry ensure that domestic and international travel figures will rise. The data cited in this chapter show that these natural forces of social and economic change suggest the development of a different population. This populace will be more likely to view and interpret behavior within the society on the basis of rationalist and positivist norms. In addition to these aspects of change, the data identify the evolution of more tolerant and open value systems, systems that show less identification with more provincial objects within the Yugoslav context. These changes suggest the presence of a citizenry with characteristics conducive to needs of community development; that is, a citizenry with the capacities needed to communicate, cooperate, and understand within the complex Yugoslav setting.

Policy-makers in Yugoslavia have been intimately concerned with the question of community-building since the close of the Second World War. Although the Partisan Liberation Movement and the crucial, formative years after the war established the framework for the development of the country, the degree of community has evolved rather hesitantly. However, the findings cited here suggest that as the rate of social and economic change invariably gathers momentum, the process of individual change may also tend to increase. This means that a citizenry with the characteristics that fit the general model will be evolving at an increasingly faster rate. And since these characteristics are the trademarks of a larger and integrated political community, then the prospects may be growing brighter as the forces of development continue.

CHAPTER V

MOBILIZATION AND VALUE CHANGE: THE EFFECT OF NATIONALITY AND DEVELOPMENTAL VARIABLES

A. *Introduction*

The previous chapter applied the model to the country-wide sample. The chapter began by viewing the 1186 respondents according to some of the individual attributes that went into the mobilization, modernism, and universalism indices, and concluded by viewing the same overall sample in terms of the three-variable model. The primary concern was not to describe and account for differences among sub-groups within Yugoslavia, but rather to identify a country-wide trend or pattern if one did in fact exist.

This chapter will attempt to identify the same sort of pattern among a number of sub-groups found within the country. This effort views representatives of the four largest Yugoslav nations and analyzes the change dynamics occurring within the value systems of these individuals. Then it delineates four more sub-populations defined according to the socio-economic environment in which an individual resides. This will ascertain whether the model outlined in the previous chapter has relevance to individuals across different nationalities and contrasting environmental settings in the Yugoslav context.[1]

Although the model received empirical support when applied to the overall population in the preceding chapter, there is still reason to reserve judgment regarding its application to sub-sectors of this heterogeneous society. Therefore, focus in this chapter will be directed toward a consideration of the change dynamics occurring within the value systems of members of a number of diverse sub-populations found within the country.

It should be mentioned at the outset that nationality and the level of socio-economic development will be used primarily as control variables within this chapter. The two variables are not well-suited for explanatory purposes because of their inherent complexity. That is, while it is justifiable to posit that mobilization encourages modern values, it would be risky to posit that a particular nationality engenders certain attitudes, even when applying the relevant controls. Slovenes may exhibit higher levels of modernization than Macedonians, but it would be misleading and risky to infer that nationality per se causes this difference. It is probably safer and more accurate to say that certain traits corresponding with nationality (e.g., behavioral norms, religious beliefs, etc.) are of causal significance. Therefore, because of their complex nature, nationality and level of development. more suited for and will be used more strictly as control variables in this chapter.

B. Controlling for County-Wide Diversity

This type of sub-sample analysis calls for some special considerations in research design. An uncontrolled survey of Yugoslav society would not yield the respondents needed for this kind of analysis. That is, within a more under-developed commune or region, the ratio of mobilized to non-mobilized individuals is likely to be considerably smaller than in some developed areas. An uncontrolled, random sample would draw, therefore, a larger percentage of mobilized respondents from Slovenia than it would from Macedonia. On the basis of figures published concerning the distribution of mass media in the country, we find that the proportion of mobilized to non-mobilized citizens is likely to be greater in the northern republics than in the southern and heartland areas (see Table 16). This variation corresponds with the general social and economic differences found among the indicators published by the federal government which show that within the more mountainous heartland and southern sections of the country, the level of social and economic development is lower. As an effect of this less developed posture, lower levels are found in terms of television, radio, and newspaper ownership and usage. These shortages, as well as the earlier noted shortages in education and travel, suggest a considerably less mobilized populace in these less developed areas.

A survey based upon an unstructured, random sample would definitely show these differences. In fact, in an empirical study of this kind, respondents from the South were characterized as considerably less exposed to communication stimuli and perhaps, as a result, less mobilized than those in the more developed sections of the country.[2] But inter-national comparison of such mobilizing characteristics is not of interest here and so a sample of this kind was neither needed nor desirable. What was required was a sample that gathered populations from each section of the country with relatively equal exposure to the primary influencing variable, that is, with similar levels of social mobilization. This requirement was fulfilled by the sampling procedures, for when the sample is viewed in this regard very similar levels of mobilization are found across each nationality grouping and environmental setting.

Therefore, it should be clear that two methods of controlling are very important to the study. The first, outlined at some length in Chapter Three, insured that similar samples (i.e., samples exhibiting relatively equal levels of mobilization) were drawn from all regions of Yugoslavia, in fact, from all twenty-four communes in the country. In this chapter another type of controlling technique will be applied to aid in the analysis of the phenomenon under investigation. By "holding constant" an individual's nationality and environmental setting, it will be possible to ascertain whether the change dynamic has application both cross-nationally and over different developmental contexts.

C. Potential Intervening Influences

What is being suggested is that one's national origin in Yugoslavia, as well as the socio-economic setting in which he resides, may affect his propensity to change in accordance with the trend outlined in the previous chapter. This outside effect may take a number of forms. First, it may affect the relationship between mobilization and traditionalism. It may be found, for example, that the size of the correlation between mobilization and modernized values is considerably higher among Slovenes. The same is possible for the modernism-universalism and mobilization-universalism linkages. Therefore, external interference can affect any of the three linkages and take one of two different forms. Namely, it may either decrease or increase the correlation between the two attributes of the individual. However, before examining the data, let us consider in somewhat greater detail the ideas of national origin and socio-economic setting within the country. This may give a better idea of the influence of these factors upon the model.

The largest South Slavic nationalities include the Serbs, Croats, Slovenes, and Macedonians. Each of these Yugoslav nationalities developed through rather different historical experiences. The Slovenes, for example, were never under the administration of the Ottoman Empire and developed rather peacefully under the Austrian crown. The Croats, on the other hand, provided the barrier to the northward expansion of the Turks, and were also exposed to different influences because of the greater Hungarian presence in this section of the Balkan lands. However, in both of these northern republics, Western domination was blended with Catholicism to ensure the evolution of two cultural types of rather marked contrast to those to be found in the South.

The southern nationalities all experienced the oppression of the Turk to a greater or lesser degree. The Macedonians were conquered first and liberated last, and in the meantime, endured over 500 years of Ottoman influence. However, in contrast to the Slavs of the heartland (now Bosnia-Hercegovina), rather limited numbers of the Macedonians were Islamized. The Serbs, proving true to their heroic and uncompromising tradition, also

TABLE 16

DISTRIBUTION OF INSTRUMENTS OF MASS MEDIA BY REPUBLIC

REPUBLIC	NUMBER OF HOUSEHOLDS PER ...		
	Radio Receiver	Television Set	Daily Newspapers Published[a]
Slovenia	1.1	2.1	2.7
Croatia	1.6	2.5	4.7
Macedonia	1.7	2.9	6.7
Serbia Proper	2.2	2.8	1.5
Vojvodina	1.6	2.2	9.5
Kosovo	4.4	7.1	15.3
Bosnia-Hercegovina	3.0	4.5	7.8
Montenegro	2.6	3.5	__b
Yugoslavia	1.9	2.8	3.2

Source: *Statistički Godišnjak Jugoslavije* 1972, pp. 509-510.

[a]Although the figures are presented for the number of newspapers printed per household in the republic, it should be noted that many newspapers are transported and read outside of the republic in which they were printed.

[b]There are no daily newspapers published within the republic of Montenegro.

endured the Turk without being absorbed. The blend between an intense desire for freedom and a strong Orthodox religious tradition ensured the preservation of a distinct Serbian type. The other Yugoslav nationalities also experienced varied historical experiences, and it can be said that all represent unique national types within the contemporary South Slavic context.

Relevant to the concern here is the fact that the historical experiences of the different national groups brought about a complex mosaic of contrasting national characteristics. These differences in national character, it is reasonable to assume, may have some effect upon the change dynamics hypothesized within the model. Stories are often heard about the national character of certain groups within the country, for example, that a certain group has a unique "style" of thinking and behaving, such as a style that may be more resistant to the changes suggested by a modernizing environment. These feelings are most often expressed by the man in the street and are usually directed toward the inhabitants of other sections of the country. However, more organized and documented, but still similar arguments are made by some of Yugoslavia's most respected anthropologists and ethnologists. Erlich, for example, speaks of the type of character that evolved in the Ottoman influenced areas in the following way:

> Many consequences of the era of Ottoman greatness as well as of the period of its decline have remained here. Among the latter are the economic backwardness, the low standard of living, and the crude conservatism, which served as a brake to technical progress and was mirrored clearly in the illiteracy of the people. The traits of the Oriental style are in sharp contrast to the tribal style: Private life is considered more important and the philosophy of life is fatalistic.[3]

Later Professor Erlich implies that this "style" may tend to resist the changes suggested by the modernizing influences outlined in previous chapters. This general idea has definite implications for the relationships hypothesized in the previous chapter. It suggests that the national populations who developed under the influence of the Orient (e.g., Bosnian and Macedonian) might be less receptive to mobilizing influences, and then, even after having been exposed to such influences, be less likely to change from more traditional and particularistic value systems.

One might contend, as Erlich implies, that because of the 500 years of Turkish domination, a mental set has evolved among the inhabitants of the South that will be resistant to the changes suggested by increased education, information, and travel. Conceivably, a resistant traditional character may have been ingrained and may be found even among the highly educated, exposed, and traveled sector of the Oriental (i.e., Ottoman) influenced areas.[4] On the other hand, a contrasting argument merits consideration: after the long history of social and economic deprivation experienced by the area, the inhabitants may be most susceptible to the changes suggested by the arrival of twentieth century technology and information flow. In effect, it may be that the Macedonian has been information "starved," and that once this "barrier" is broken, and he starts reading, viewing, and traveling at increasing rates, the change in values will follow at a more than proportionate rate.[5]

The members of other national groups in Yugoslavia present interesting contrasts to the historical development and contemporary posture of the Macedonians. The Slovenes, for example, were never reached by the cultural influences and administrative domination of the Ottomans and, therefore, developed rather differently under the Habsburg crown. The economic, social and political consequences of this development are generally clear, but less is known about the nature of the attitudinal systems characterizing that population. Perhaps a set of values has evolved among the Slovenes that is more resistant to the changes suggested in the previous chapter. Also, there may be certain qualities within the Slovene character that restrict the possibilities for disengagement from the more particular-istic attachments within the Slovene setting.

The Serbs and Croats also raise a number of questions in this regard. The two groups represent the two dominant nationalities in the country and possess features that might suggest some interference with the linkages found within the model. Both groups developed through distinct historical traditions of their own and are usually thought of as representing contrast-ing national types. The Croats represent a product of the Western world with a strong Catholic heritage, while the Serbs endured under the influ-ence of the East and retained their strong Orthodox tradition. Both have a strong sense of national pride and are intent on maintaining their national identity. Hoffman and Neal reveal a relevant characteristic of the Serbs in the following quotation:

> Serbian nationalism, in which the Kosovo legend has played such an important role, did not die with the medieval Serbian state. It was kept alive chiefly by the Serbian Orthodox Church. A mer-ger of religion and nationalism resulted which was perhaps more complete than any before or since, not excluding the relation-ship of the Russian Orthodox Church to Russian nationalism.[6]

This kind of merger between the religious and the temporal, and the feel-ings that emanate from it, suggest belief systems capable of interfering with the universalism variable. The analysis will attempt to determine if national identity and pride ensure attachments to more provincial objects regardless of mobilization and modernization levels.

In his excellent study of one Serbian village, Halpern suggests that na-tional pride plays an important role in the life of the Serbs. He writes:

> The patriotism and pride exhibited by the Orasani are character-istic of all Serbs. They feel themselves to be much more than simply inhabitants of Serbia. They are the creators and defenders of their country . . . This binding identity with their homeland has been re-inforced over generations by the chanting of heroic epic poems, instilling in almost every child a knowledge of, and love for, his country (i.e., Serbia) which he retains throughout his life.[7]

Perhaps this intense patriotism toward and identity with Serbian based symbols will override the effects attributed to the mobilization and modernism variables.

The Croatian identity might also be characterized as a merger between church, tradition, and national pride, and also raises questions about move-ments toward a less particularistic value system. The Croat data, for exam-ple, may confirm the link between mobilization and more modern values, but show no relationship between these two attributes and levels of parti-cularism. In other words, particularism or its absence may be a character-istic of the Croats that has no relationship to the mobilizing and modernizing forces. Since nationality is crucial enough in Yugoslav society to suggest intervening tendencies to the change phenomenon, the model will be applied individually to the four largest national groups in the country—the Slovenes, Serbs, Croats, and Macedonians—to test the research hypotheses in greater detail.[8]

It was also suggested earlier that the socio-economic environment in which an individual finds himself may influence his propensity for value change in accordance with the model. The suggestion implies that the environmental setting in which an individual lives and works may have some relationship to his readiness and susceptibility for value change. In an area of extreme social and economic deprivation, increases in levels of social mobilization among a small segment of the population may have little effect on separating them from the more traditional ways of life. Namely, within an extremely deprived community, such as our sampled communes of Nevesinje in Bosnia-Hercegovina, or Osečina in Serbia, the proportion of citizens reached by the mobilizing forces is extremely small.[9] While contrastingly, the mobilized citizens found in a developed, urban community, such as Medveščak in Zagreb or Zvezdara in Belgrade, are likely to find themselves comprising an overwhelming percentage of the population.

It may be that mobilization per se is less likely to affect the individual in Nevesinje or Osečina. Although the individual in such a commune may be reached by modernizing stimuli, the people closely surrounding him are not, generally speaking, so mobilized. As a result, the "unmobilized" sector of the community may tend to have a restraining effect upon the hypothesized changes in the value systems of the mobilized citizens. For example, while the mobilized young man of Osečina may have gone to the university at Belgrade, earned a diploma, returned to the community, and now lives the life-style of a "mobilized" citizen, this change may bring about meager changes in his value system due to the environmental effects of the community. Contrastingly, the inhabitant of the upper income area within Belgrade is likely to find himself "mobilized " along with the rest of the community and therefore finds fewer outside or contextual restraints upon his changing value system. In short, it is suggested that the milieu in which an individual finds himself may affect his propensity to change once he is reached by the mobilizing influences.[10]

D. Cross-National Comparisons—
The Slovene, Croat, Serb, and Macedonian Samples

We now come to the most important part of the analysis where we compare the relationships across national units by applying the model to representatives of the four largest nations in the country. This will be done in order to ascertain whether there is something about one's nationality in Yugoslavia which affects the relationship found among the overall sample.[11]

Members of the Slovene nationality, who reside in the northern-most section of the country and developed under the economically more favorable conditions of Western influence, display relationships that show a slight "reaction" to the value change found among the larger sample and registered in Figure 6. Namely, all three linkages illustrate a rather substantial decrease in strength among representatives of this nationality (see Figure 9). While a *gamma* coefficient of .40 was found between A and B within the overall sample, one of considerably weaker strength (.31) is shown for the Slovenes.[12] The forces of mobilization, then, are of lesser importance in changing traditional value sets among the Slovenes than they are for the average member of the overall sample. In fact, the forces are weaker in regard to the Slovenes than among any other nationality. At the same time, however, it is necessary to note that members of this sub-population represent the most modern nationality in the country when viewing the percentage breakdown on the traditionalism-modernism scale. While 66 per cent of the Slovene respondents rank on the "modern side" of the scale, only 53 percent of the Croats, 51 per cent of the Serbs, and 40 per cent of the Macedonians rank as clearly modern.[13]

FIGURE 9

THREE VARIABLE MODEL: SLOVENES

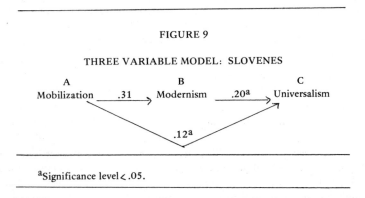

[a]Significance level < .05.

At first sight, the Slovene posture appears to present somewhat of a paradox in regard to the mobilization-modernism linkage. Namely, although mobilization is significantly related to modernism among Slovenes, the .31 *gamma* coefficient indicates that the influencing strength of the mobilization forces is of less power in bringing about modern values than among most other nationalities.[14] Yet, as indicated above, the Slovenes reflect the most modern values in the country. The explanation, however, may be quite simple. It might be contended that although mobilization helps one to become modern in Slovenia, it is certainly not the only channel. The relatively high level of modernism may result from the long and impressive tradition of favorable development within the republic. This highly developed socio-economic environment may have a tendency to encourage modern values even among segments of the population missed by the mobilizing influences. Hence, the mobilization-modernism linkage illustrates a relatively weak coefficient.

When moving to the next most important link within the model (i.e., B-C), it is found that one's posture on the modernism scale is of relatively minor significance in predicting whether or not the individual will be universalistic. Clearly, a Slovene can be particularistic and at the same time possess a modern system of beliefs. In fact, while it was earlier noted that Slovenes were the most modern ethnic group in the country, now it must be pointed out that they rank second to the Macedonians in terms of being "most particularistic." While 45 per cent of the Serbs, and 52 per cent of the Croats rank as particularistic, 60 per cent of the Slovenes and 73 per cent of the Macedonians rank on the particularistic side of the scale.[15]

What is it about the character and nature of the Slovene nationality that limits their ability to disengage from a close identification with more personal and provincial attachments even after having attained a modern set of values? A closer consideration of the evolution and present position of the nation may be instructive at this point. The historical development of Slovenia produced a cultural style that closely reflects what might be identified as the most "Western type" within the South Slavic context.[16] Perhaps the Slovenes fear that this national type is being threatened and in danger of being lost because of the relatively small size of the nation.[17] Understandably, in order to preserve their culture, as they and all other Yugoslav nationalities are intent on doing, the Slovenes must guard against and preserve the basic elements upon which this culture is based. Clearly, the elements represented in the particularism-universalism scale (i.e., language, nationality, locale, family history, and value systems) are crucial bases of that culture. Hence, even the most modern Slovene has trouble disengaging from these elements since such disengagement might reasonably be interpreted by the individual as representing a threat to his national identity. The larger, more dominant nationalities like the Serbs and Croats, on the other hand, may perceive the situation in a somewhat less fearful fashion because of their larger numbers.[18]

The important point for consideration at this juncture is perhaps not that Slovenes are considerably more particularistic than Croats and Serbs— but rather, in view of the Slovene's relatively high level of modernized values, a less particularistic posture might have been expected on the basis of the relationships suggested in the model. This presents a number of important implications for the community-building process within the country. First, a population is identified within Slovenia that is certainly mobilized within the Yugoslav context, a population that has access to relatively high levels of information stimuli. This characteristic as well as the impressive tradition of socio-economic success in the Slovene republic have brought about the most modernized national population in the country. However, both of these characteristics have been somewhat unsuccessful in drawing the Slovene away from the more private, provincial concerns of his own culture. As a result, it is suggested that even as social and economic development continues, the Slovene will tend to cling to these concerns and, in doing so, restrict his ability to view Yugoslav concerns in a manner that will be conducive to the further evolution of a larger socialist community.

The Croats, however, closely reflect and further verify the relationships found among representatives of the country-wide sample (see Figure 10). In fact, they illustrate an even stronger relationship between the mobilizing forces and modernizing values than was noted previously for the overall sample. The model clearly reveals that as the natural forces of development bring about a more mobilized Croatian citizenry, increasingly higher levels of modernism and universalism can be expected.

FIGURE 10

THREE VARIABLE MODEL: CROATS

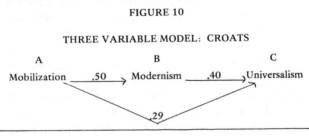

This general pattern does not necessarily imply that Croats will become less protective and sensitive about their own economic development, or that their desires for an even greater level of decentralization and autonomy will suddenly begin to subside. However, the findings seem to suggest that such interests may be perceived and presented in a rather different political style. First, the scale of modern values showed that the individual Croat may be more inclined to view events and relations within his society on the basis of rationalist and positivist norms. Furthermore, the scale constructed from potentially particularistic elements in the Yugoslav context illustrates that with further mobilization and modernization, the Croat will tend to disengage himself at an increasing rate from these more provincial attachments. In short, this process of individual change seems to suggest the evolution of a different system of values defining the setting in which political, social, and economic action takes place.[19] Again, it must be stressed that this does not suggest an absence or dissolution of political questions, but rather a different setting in which these questions are perceived, considered and contested. The two populations examined thus far—although exhibiting certain differences—illustrate a process of value change that may be establishing this new political setting. In illustrating this pattern, they correspond with the trend identified among the larger sample.[20]

The Serbs also tend to reflect the same changes as found in the overall sample. However, there is a minor weakening in the first linkage of the model suggesting a somewhat lower change capability of mobilization within the Serbian context (see Figure 11). This general resistance to modernizing values among Serbs might be viewed as a function of the tendency for members of this nationality to find themselves in less developed

FIGURE 11

THREE VARIABLE MODEL: SERBS

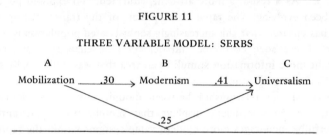

A   B   C

Mobilization ____.30___→ Modernism ____.41___→ Universalism

.25

environs.[21] For example, while 96 per cent of Slovenes in the sample find themselves in highly developed environs, only 13 per cent of the Serbs reside in similar settings. While the mobilized Serb may have the attributes tending to encourage a more rationalist and positivist orientation (i.e., a more modern set of values), the environment in which he finds himself may tend to restrict the value changes that engender a more modern orientation.

In regard to the B-C linkage in the model, a close association is shown between modern and universalistic value configurations. In fact, the coefficient is the same as found for the overall sample. The third linkage, mobilization-universalism, shows the same weak, hypothesized influence of mobilization and corresponds with what has already been ascertained about the larger sample.

The most southern and last nationality we will consider in the country, the Macedonians, illustrate stronger linkages than any nationality considered in the analysis (see Figure 12). All coefficients are considerably above those found in the larger sample. The first linkage represented in the model, i.e., mobilization-modernism, seems to support what might be called an "information-starved" thesis. Macedonia, although always rich in

FIGURE 12

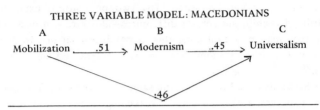

THREE VARIABLE MODEL: MACEDONIANS

material and human resources, has only recently begun tapping its abundant supplies. The general industrialization and socio-economic development that has followed, along with the vigorous efforts of the entire country, have greatly improved the level of social and economic subsistence in the area. As a result, a more affluent, educated, and exposed population has been evolving. The rapid development of the transportation system also has ensured that this increasingly sophisticated population is traveling more. These socio-economic and demographic changes have inevitably brought more information stimuli to an area that was traditionally sheltered. The impinging stimulus in turn displays its effect when viewing the strength of the relationship between mobilization and modernism. In short, the .51 coefficient displays that mobilization significantly and powerfully encourages more modern value systems within the representatives of this Macedonian control group.

It should not be forgotten that Macedonians are still, relatively speaking, the most traditional of the four national populations considered in this study. But it must also be noted that they probably had the longest way to go. In other words, because of historical realities, the Macedonia of post-World War II Yugoslavia represented one of the most traditional sectors in the country. However, the rate of change suggested by the mobilizing forces indicates that they will be one of the populations with the highest rate of change as the inevitable process of mobilization continues.

The relationship between modernism and universalism is also considerably stronger among Macedonians when compared with other populations (see Figure 12). Again, the reader is reminded that the Macedonians are the most particularistic national group identified in this study. But perhaps of more importance is the finding that the extent of particularism-universalism among Macedonians is correlated very highly with modern values. Therefore, if the inevitable increase of mobilization will continue to reduce levels of traditionalism in the manner that the data suggest, their rates of particularism should also continue to fall. In a sense then, Macedonians have the longest way to go in terms of becoming more modernized and universalistic, but will tend to move faster due to an intensified process of mobilization.

The linkage between mobilization and universalism (A—C) also shows surprising strength among the Macedonians. Earlier, and incidently for every national sample considered in the study, the A—C link was substantially lower than the A—B (mobilization—modernism) and B—C (modernism—universalism) linkages. Among the Macedonians, however, mobilization is of considerable importance to the development of both modern and universal values and the intermediating role of modernized values is minimized. Within this population, then, the stimuli gained through increased mobilization are definitely the moving forces.

After having viewed the "within-systems" relationships among the four largest nationalities in Yugoslavia, two major findings are clear. First, the three variable model of individual change had general application and was relatively consistent across all four populations. Although the intensity of the linkages varied somewhat, a general verification of the Yugoslav's developmental logic was found among the two more westernized, Catholicized populations from the North, the Orthodox Serbs from the interior regions, and the "easternized" sample from Macedonia. Overall, the model displayed its cross-national application.

The second major finding pertains to the differential relationships and contrasting change dynamics that were registered across the representatives of the four Yugoslav nations. The data showed, for example, that the forces of mobilization and modernized values exhibit somewhat weaker capabilities in drawing the Slovene away from more particularistic value patterns. Contrastingly, among representatives of the other three major nationalities and particularly in the case of the Macedonians, the data confirmed that increases in mobilization lead to more than significant increases in levels of modernism. These two phenomena, in turn, were powerfully linked to rates of disengagement from more private and provincial attachments among representatives of the Croat, Serb, and Macedonian control groups.

E. Communal Comparisons
Controlling for Level of Socio-Economic Development

The 1186 respondents will now be classified according to the commune in which they reside. The communes are categorized on the basis of the level of socio-economic development characterizing this local governmental unit. A consideration of the ranking of communes shows that they range from the highly developed industrial center of Maribor in Slovenia to the almost "untouched" village of Nevesinje in the southern-most reaches of Bosnia-Hercegovina. By assigning quartile rankings to the twenty-four communes, the following breakdown is achieved:

I. Highly Developed	Commune	Cultural-Region[22]
	Maribor	Slovenia
	Medveščak	Croatia (Zagreb)
	Zvezdara	Serbia (Belgrade)
	Novo Mesto	Slovenia
	Šibenik	Adriatic Coastal (Croatia)
	Cerknica	Slovenia
II. Developed	Herceg Novi	Adriatic Coastal (Montenegro)
	Slavonski Brod	Croatia
	Srebobran	Vojvodina (Serbia)
	Svetozarevo	Serbia
	Cetinje	Montenegro
	Titov Veles	Macedonia
III. Less Developed	Čakovec	Croatia
	Ohrid	Macedonia
	Duga Resa	Croatia
	Lukavac	Bosnia-Hercegovina
	Brač	Adriatic Coastal (Croatia)
	Gospić	Croatia
IV. Least Developed	Vranje	Serbia
	Jajce	Bosnia-Hercegovina
	Peć	Kosovo (Serbia)
	Radoviš	Macedonia
	Osečina	Serbia
	Nevesinje	Bosnia-Hercegovina

The highly developed category (I) is represented by three Slovenian communes, two urban communes drawn from Zagreb and Belgrade, and a developing industrial center on the Adriatic Coast. The developed category (II) draws communes from almost all sections of the country with each representing a thriving industrial center within its particular territory. The less developed group (III) represents three predominantly agricultural communes from some of the most deprived sections in Croatia, in addition to the rocky island of Brač which is just beginning to develop some of its tourist potentials, and includes agricultural communes from Macedonia and Bosnia-Hercegovina. The least developed communes (IV) are drawn from either Orthodox or *Muslimani* influenced areas and represent some of the most economically deprived communities in the country.

It was ascertained earlier that higher levels of educational attainment, travel, and mass media exposure exist in the more highly developed communes.[23] Therefore, the ratio of mobilized to non-mobilized individuals will inevitably be greater within the more developed and affluent settings. Because of the higher percentage of mobilized inhabitants in these communes, it is reasonable to suggest that the effect of mobilization forces upon value change among individuals in these environments will be somewhat greater. The suggestion implies that value change may be more likely when the values of surrounding people are changing also or have been changed already.

When viewing the most developed category, the coefficients show that the relationship between mobilization and modernism is somewhat higher and that between modernism and universalism somewhat lower than those found among the overall sample (see Figure 13). It must be remembered in this regard that the most developed category is dominated by the three communes from Slovenia and thus will reflect the general Slovene posture noted in the foregoing section. That is, modernism and universalism were rather weakly related among the Slovene sample, with this posture seen in

FIGURE 13

THREE VARIABLE MODEL: INDIVIDUALS INHABITING
MOST DEVELOPED COMMUNES

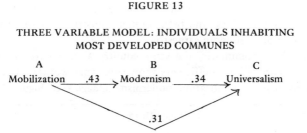

the somewhat weaker relationship between B and C (.34) for this collection of communes. Outside of this minor exception the communes representing highly developed environments closely parallel the country-wide pattern.

In the category representing "developed" communes, particularly strong coefficients are found between each of the variables (see Figure 14).

FIGURE 14

THREE VARIABLE MODEL: INDIVIDUALS INHABITING
DEVELOPED COMMUNES

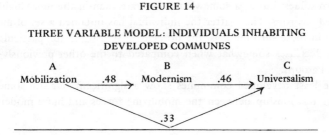

This finding takes on special importance when one considers the composition of this grouping of communes. Namely, within its ranks a commune is found representing almost every culture region in the country. Yet all are characterized by a common and relatively high industrializing environment, and as the data suggest, a strong pattern of individual change. That is, the populations drawn from these industrializing communes exhibit strong relationships between the mobilizing forces and modernizing values, and further, between such values and those de-emphasizing aspects of particularism in the Yugoslav context.

The less developed category represents deprived agricultural communities. It should be noted that two of these communities are beginning to develop rather rapidly because of the recent increase in Yugoslavia's tourist activity. Brač, an island off the coast from the thriving Dalmatian city of Split, and Ohrid, an isolated community on the edge of one of Yugoslavia's most beautiful lakes, are likely to be influenced rather heavily by increasing tourist trade and can expect their environments to be affected accordingly. At present, however, they still are in a transitional stage of development. The economic future of the remaining four communities appears more unchanging and the modernizing characteristics may be considerably more difficult to attain. All were at one time predominantly agricultural communities, and their limited industrial potential have only recently been pursued more earnestly.

Within these communes, the same country-wide pattern is found although the correlation coefficients show somewhat weaker relationships, particularly in the mobilization-modernism linkage (see Figure 15). This

FIGURE 15

THREE VARIABLE MODEL: INDIVIDUALS INHABITING
LESS DEVELOPED COMMUNES

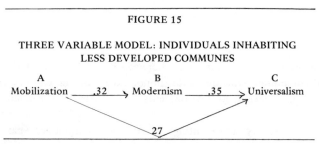

figure suggests that the mobilized person does, as usual, reflect more modern values, but at a somewhat lower rate than in the more highly developed environs. Then, after the individual has obtained a set of modern beliefs in these surroundings, the propensity to assume non-particularistic values decreases somewhat when compared to the other previously-cited control groups.

The least developed communes show a significant but still somewhat weaker relationship between the mobilizing forces and more modernized beliefs (see Figure 16). This collection of communes represents two predominantly "Islamized" communities in Bosnia-Hercegovina, a predominantly Albanian community in Kosovo, an isolated Macedonian village, and two under-developed Serbian communities. Overall, they represent a deprived collection of small Yugoslav communities located in conservative Orthodox and Moslem areas.

FIGURE 16

THREE VARIABLE MODEL: INDIVIDUALS INHABITING
LEAST DEVELOPED COMMUNES

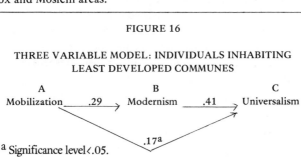

The general conservative tendency found in these areas seems to express itself, as suggested by Erlich and others, in the mobilization-modernism linkage of the model. The weaker coefficient suggests that mobilization per se has less influence in breaking traditional value systems and, furthermore, overcoming universalism among inhabitants of these areas. However, the .41 coefficient registered for the B—C linkage suggests that once an inhabitant of these communes has attained a modern belief system, his tendency to assume non-particularistic values is of the same probabilities as among the larger sample. Therefore, the problem resides in the crucial A—B relationship. Clearly, mobilization as the initial variable in the causal chain does not exert the same changing powers in these conservative, less developed environments.

Therefore, the findings drawn from this section show that contrasting environmental settings exert a significant differential effect upon the phenomena of individual change. Although the general cumulative trend among the variables holds throughout all settings, a considerably stronger association between the mobilizing forces and modern beliefs was found in the more highly developed communes. Whereas coefficients of .43 and .48 were registered for the A—B linkages among the two collections of more developed communes, considerably weaker coefficients of .32 and .29 were found for the two collections of less-developed communes. Furthermore, the same general weakening of the mobilization forces was found in the mobilization-universalism linkage among respondents drawn from these less developed communes. Accordingly, it can be concluded that the isolated and historically "backward" setting of the less-developed communes exerts a restraining effect upon the change tendencies suggested by increased education, mass media exposure, and domestic and internal travel.

However, it is also important to note that the findings drawn from this section support the general application of the study's conception of individual change in all environmental settings. Mobilization, modernism, and universalism are relevant indicators of change not only in urbanized metropolitan centers and thriving industrialized sections of the country, but also represent and empirically identify a process of change that is occurring in the many diverse Yugoslav settings. In short, education, information, and travel engender a similar pattern of value change irrespective of environmental setting.

CHAPTER VI

PATTERNS OF MOBILIZATION AND CHANGE TENDENCY

A. *Introduction*

The preceding chapter viewed the phenomenon of individual change across groups possessing relatively equal exposure to the initial influencing variable. The sample design allowed investigation of eight separate control groups which displayed rather similar levels of social mobilization. The data confirmed that the mobilizing forces encouraged value change within each of the four national groups and four environmental settings. This finding may have been interpreted to indicate that the change process is sweeping the entire society and that all individuals have a relatively equal chance of being reached by the change stimuli. However, this should not be inferred from the findings. The data simply indicate that mobilized individuals exist within all nationalities and environmental settings, and further, that these individuals are more inclined toward value change than non-mobilized citizens.

This chapter will move somewhat beyond this. First, it will attempt to determine who these mobilized individuals are likely to be. For example, are they more likely to represent the young or the old, elites or masses, Communist party members or non-members? Then, after making this determination, the chapter will investigate the change phenomenon within each of these groups. Supposedly, at least some members of these different sectors are reached by change stimuli. However, are the value systems of these members likely to be affected in similar ways after having acquired these mobilizing characteristics?

Therefore, the chapter will address itself to two objectives. First, it will consider what sectors of Yugoslav society are most likely to be reached by the impetus for value change. Secondly, it will consider whether the change phenomenon is similar once the stimulus has been received. The first objective requires an analysis of distribution and the second a consideration of the propensity for change.

The conceptualizations of Deutsch and others suggest that the processes of individual change are closely related to the forces of mobilization. They imply that the individual reached by the change stimuli is likely to display different political attitudes and behavior than the individual missed by the same influences. Therefore, it seems important to ascertain what sectors of

Yugoslav society are more likely to be characterized by high levels of education, mass media exposure, and domestic and international travel. By doing so, a better idea of the breadth and scope of the change process can be gained.

Age will be considered first to see if mobilization characteristics are more likely to be found among some age sectors of Yugoslavia than others. One might reason that older sectors would naturally have had more time to attain further education, to travel widely, and perhaps acquire the resources necessary to own the instruments necessary for broader mass media exposure. However, it should also be argued that these phenomena (i.e., education, exposure, and wide travel) are more likely to be characteristic of the post-war generations.

The figures presented in Table 17 illustrate that the distribution of mobilization does vary somewhat within each of the three age groups (see Table 17). The variation, however, does not occur in a linear manner as the percentage distributions and *gamma* coefficient indicate. On the contrary, the figures indicate that the differences seem to follow a curvilinear pattern which can be identified by viewing the cells containing a majority of respondents in each age group. That is, the majority of the "55 and over" group are low on mobilization, the majority of the "34-35" group are high, and a predominance of the "18-33" group are found at medium levels. This curvilinear pattern suggests that the overwhelming majority (75 per cent) of the youngest sector have yet to attain high levels. The middle-aged sector, on the other hand, apparently possesses the time and resources necessary to attain this highest level, while the oldest category might be characterized as "retreatist" or "isolationist" due to the predominance of its number in the low category.

TABLE 17

AGE OF RESPONDENT BY LEVEL OF MOBILIZATION

AGE	LEVEL OF MOBILIZATION[a]			
	(*percentages*)			
	Low	Medium	High	N
18-33	33	42	25	479
34-54	38	22	40	415
55 and over	41	26	33	278
Total	35	33	32	1172

Gamma = .00   Sig. $<$.05

[a]The original nine-point Social Mobilization Index has been collapsed into low, medium, and high categories for convenience of presentation in this section.

The figures presented in Table 17 point to another rather important phenomenon. Namely, the groups (especially those drawn from the two older sectors) illustrate that the resource (i.e., mobilization) is rather "polarized" within the society. In fact, the two older groups show a predominance of their members in the two extreme (i.e., low and high) categories. This seems to point to the presence of a gap between the "haves" and "have nots." Some individuals appear to have been exposed to relatively large amounts of information stimuli, while others seem to have been isolated. The next variable gives a good idea of who these individuals are likely to be.

By considering the socio-political status of the 1186 respondents, it is possible to view the distribution of mobilization characteristics among "elite" and "mass" sectors of the society.[1] When the overall sample is viewed in this regard, the data show that individuals in elite positions are much more likely to be characterized by high levels of mobilizing influences than are those in the mass sectors (see Table 18). While almost no elites are found with low levels of mobilization, the overwhelming majority (70 per cent) of the low-status sector fall into the lowest category. This suggests that the mobilizing process is primarily an "elitist phenomenon," a phenomenon with one over-riding implication for this study. Namely, because it is extremely difficult and unusual for the masses to find themselves exposed to the mobilization stimuli, ensuing changes in value systems may be unlikely.[2]

TABLE 18

SOCIAL AND POLITICAL STATUS
BY LEVEL OF MOBILIZATION

STATUS	LEVEL OF MOBILIZATION			
	(percentages)			
	Low	Medium	High	N
Masses	70	27	3	597
Social Cultural Elites	0	36	64	334
Political Elites	1	39	60	238
Total	35	33	32	1169

Gamma = .75 Sig. > .001

The data suggest that the phenomenon of individual change and potential for community-building may be more relevant to the elite sectors of the society than to the rank and file masses. Even though it may be found

that the masses are as receptive to the value changes suggested by mobilization, they are not being reached. Hence, the belief systems equipping the
individual for further community development are more often found
among the elite sectors. The result may be a differential effect in the
community-building process, with higher rates and wider change tending
to be found among the sectors representing high status positions.

Earlier formulations described the mobilizing characteristics as an
extremely valuable resource due to its ability to engender value change.
Now it should be noted that it is not only valuable, but in a developing
country such as Yugoslavia, it is also relatively scarce. Therefore, those
with access to the stimuli find themselves in control of an important developmental resource. This control may mean faster and broader value
change and perhaps a growing gap between the belief systems of the
"haves" and the "have nots." The low status agricultural workers found in
the isolated, outlying areas, and even the factor workers found in the industrializing urban environments, find themselves at a disadvantage. One
might expect the result to display itself in the establishment of the prerequisites among the elite sectors for community-development and a more
unchanging, static posture among the masses.

Two solutions to the problem are envisioned within the developing
Yugoslav context. First, developmental trends show a decrease in the number of occupational positions exhibiting a general isolation from the stimuli. Whereas over three-fourths of the population depended upon agriculture for their incomes before the Second World War, less than half do so
today. In effect, increasingly larger sectors of the society are finding themselves in positions characterized by higher mobilization. The second solution to the increasing differentiation involves a concerted effort on the
part of the regime to make mobilization a mass phenomenon. However,
since the agricultural and other lower status sectors will exist as a sizable
portion of the total work force for some years to come, efforts will have
to be made to mobilize these individuals if the regime is interested in closing the gap. In fact, the system has been showing vigorous efforts to do
just that by increasing education, mass media facilities, and cultural contact among these sectors.[3] In effect, then, both solutions are at work today.

The data presented in the next table show whether or not this difference in distribution is also carried over into the Yugoslav League of Communists. On the basis of the previous table, we might expect higher levels
of mobilization among Party members since they naturally tend to find
themselves in positions of social and political leadership. The data indicate
that this is the case with the Party member sector exhibiting considerably
more individuals with high levels of mobilization than the non-member
group (see Table 19).

Therefore, just as in the case of social and political elites, the data indicate that members of the Yugoslav League of Communists have had greater access to the mobilization agents. This has of course important implications concerning the growth of community among different sectors of the society. Since it was suggested earlier that mobilization is likely to be an important resource equipping individuals with the value configurations likely to engender the further development of community, the potential for this growth process would appear to be greater within elite and party sectors of the society.

The higher levels of mobilization found within the elite and party member groups suggest reciprocal causation. Increased education, information, and travel equip some individuals for elite positions and then, after assuming the position, these individuals are likely to attain even greater levels of the resources because of the nature and responsibilities of the position.

TABLE 19

MEMBERSHIP IN
THE YUGOSLAV LEAGUE OF COMMUNISTS
BY LEVEL OF MOBILIZATION

MEMBERSHIP	LEVEL OF MOBILIZATION			
	(*percentages*)			
	Low	Medium	High	N
Non-Members	52	30	18	628
Party-Members	17	36	47	548
Total	35	33	32	1176

Gamma = .64   Sig. > .001

Namely, elites are required to follow the mass media and are traveling widely because of the responsibilities of their positions. This reciprocal pattern and the inevitable result of a highly mobilized elite is likely to display itself in the further differentiation between the elite and mass sectors irrespective of the Yugoslav efforts mentioned above.

B. Mobilization and Attitude Change: Applying the Controls

In this section, the change pattern will be compared across the different control groups by referring again to the three variable model. The section considers mobilization and the propensity for change within groups based upon age, social-political status, and Communist party membership. The data will show whether the various control groups possess certain qualities capable of "over-riding" or changing the relationships found earlier among the overall sample. The data will illustrate, for example, whether there is something about the more elderly, the lower status rank and file masses, or those who are not members of the Communist party, that weakens the correlations found earlier among the country-wide sample.

Attitude Change Among Different Age Groups

Conceivably, the age of a Yugoslav might affect his readiness for or resistance to value change. It seems reasonable to suspect that older Yugoslavs may have greater difficulty in accepting more modern and universalistic value sets even though they may have traveled widely, been exposed to the mass media, and perhaps attained relatively high levels of education. Socialization theory notes that attitude change is generally easier and less restricted among the younger sectors of a society.[4] This basic and now well-documented finding would suggest that when applying the same mobilizing stimuli to a young and old subject, the rate of change would be faster and greater among the younger. If this is the case, stronger relationships will be found between variables in the model for younger sectors of the sample.

It should be noted that with further industrialization in Yugoslavia, considerable numbers are moving from the hinterlands to the population centers for the primary purpose of taking new jobs in the factories. The movement of whole families presents an interesting case illustrating the potential significance of the age variable to the model. For example, cases of father and son moving and accepting new jobs in the same factory are not uncommon. They may work under the same conditions, begin to attend the Workers' University, read the same newspaper, and in general, find themselves exposed to the same mobilizing influences. However, it may be found that their age differences will suggest a differential effect as regards value change resulting from the same mobilization factors. An examination of the data will show whether such an effect exists.

The younger sub-group, representing all individuals in the sample between 18 and 33 years of age, exhibits coefficients very similar to those found for the overall population (see Group I, Table 20). Therefore, the associations between mobilized characteristics and value configurations do not appear to be affected when moving from the overall sample to the youngest control group. As suggested earlier, higher coefficients might have been expected on the basis of former empirical studies that have found a higher propensity for change among younger sectors of the populace. However, among the Yugoslav sample this does not appear to be the case.

TABLE 20

COEFFICIENTS SUMMARIZING RELATIONSHIPS
FOR THREE AGE GROUPS*

AGE GROUPS	Three Relationships		
	Mobilization-Modernism (A → B)	Modernism-Universalism (B → C)	Mobilization-Universalism (A → C)
Group I: 18-33 Years	.38	.36	.28
Group II: 34-53 Years	.40	.36	.30
Group III: Over 53 Years	.37	.49	.25

*For purposes of presentation in this table, as well as those to follow, we have simply drawn the correlation coefficients from the three variable model for each control group and listed them together in the table.

When considering that sector of the sample between 34 and 53 years of age, an almost identical set of correlation coefficients is found (see Table 20). Mobilization as a change stimuli exhibits the same relationship to value configurations in both control groups. Therefore, the age of a respondent does not appear to impede or encourage the cumulative effect of the variables among the two younger groups.

The oldest sector of the sample lends further support to the absence of any interference that might have been attributed to the age variable (see Table 20). One slight difference is found in this group, however, and it concerns the modernism-universalism link in the model. Within the oldest control group, modernism and universalism are somewhat more closely related. This slightly stronger relationship suggests that a modern set of values is of somewhat greater power in encouraging universalistic values in this sector of the sample.

The most important finding drawn from this consideration of three different age sectors in Yugoslavia is the general strength and consistency of the phenomena across all three groups. The data indicate that once an individual is reached by the mobilizing agents, he is likely to reflect more modern and universalistic values irrespective of his age, and the propensity to reflect such values is likely to be of the same probabilities for all age sectors within the society.[5]

Attitude Change Among Different Socio-Political Status Groups

The data cited earlier showed that Yugoslavs of low social and political status are less likely to be reached by the mobilizing agents. In fact, none of the 597 citizens classified in the rank and file mass category attained the highest of the nine categories evaluating mobilization. Because of the predominance of "masses" in the low categories and a predominance of the elites in high categories, it was necessary to collapse the original nine-point mobilization index to form three larger categories. For the same reason—that is, elites in the low categories and masses in the high—the six-point modernism and universalism scales were collapsed to form three category scales.[6] This strategy allowed analysis of the influencing effect of the mobilization agents. In other words, even though a relatively small number of the rank and file masses in the sample were reached by the mobilization variable, a large enough sample is attained by collapsing to permit statistical analysis.

The group composed of individuals holding positions of political leadership, as well as the group composed of social and cultural elites, reflect relatively the same linkages between the A-B and B-C combinations as found among the broader Yugoslav populace (see Group I, Table 21). Hence, Yugoslav elites show no general reaction to or fostering of the change phenomena suggested for those linkages. Even though members of the elite groups are more likely to have access to the mobilization stimuli than the rank and file masses, their linkages between these two sets of variables show no greater propensity for modern or universalistic values. However, the contrast in coefficients registered for the A-C relationship (political elites indicate .30 and social elites .11) suggests a significant difference between the two elite groups in Yugoslav society. Namely, mobilization per se exhibits considerably less influence upon the set of universalistic values among the collection of social and cultural elites than among the political sector. The explanation seems relevant to the contrasting positions members of these two groups hold in Yugoslav society. Namely, it may be more difficult for social and cultural elites (composed of educators, religious leaders, writers, artists, and so forth) to disengage from more particularistic orientations because such orientations are so closely tied to their professions. For example, since the importance of religion is closely aligned with nationality, region, and language differences in Yugoslavia, it would be difficult for a priest to disassociate from such orientations or attachments without denying the importance of religion. The same is true of course for editors of cultural journals, for writers, and others. Political elites, however, are inclined to reflect the ideology of the system and, therefore, tend to possess universalistic orientations at a rate more closely aligned with their mobilization levels.

The third control group to be viewed here included those individuals holding positions without any significant social, political, or cultural status. Earlier, when considering the distribution of mobilization in the society,

TABLE 21

COEFFICIENTS SUMMARIZING RELATIONSHIPS
FOR THREE SOCIO-POLITICAL STATUS GROUPS

SOCIO-POLITICAL STATUS GROUPS	Three Relationships		
	Mobilization-Modernism $(A \rightarrow B)$	Modernism-Universalism $(B \rightarrow C)$	Mobilization-Universalism $(A \rightarrow C)$
Group I: Political Elites	.40	.36	.30
Group II: Social and Cultural Elites	.34	.42	.11
Group III: Masses	.30	.50	.31

the data indicated that very small numbers of this group had been exposed to the mobilization influences.[7] However, even though they have been "denied" access (relatively speaking) to the mobilization resources in the past, this part of the study is concerned with their propensity for change once the stimuli are received. Fortunately, the sample yields enough respondents in the mass group with mobilization to statistically consider the propensity for change. When the data are examined in this respect the masses are found to be just as susceptible to value change as most other control groups (see Table 21). In fact, the .50 coefficient registered for the B-C relationship suggests that modernized and universalistic values are more closely related among this sector than the other two control groups. This means that once a modern value set can be effected among a representative of this sector, universalistic values tend to result at a more than significant rate. In short, the finding suggests that if the mobilization forces could be carried to the lower status rank and file masses, value change would follow in accordance with the now well-established pattern.

This finding suggests that the differentiation noted in the preceding footnote between elite and mass elements in Yugoslavia is not attributable to any inherent characteristics within the particular sub-populations, e.g., that villagers possess qualities impeding any movement toward more modernized and universalistic value sets. On the contrary, the data show that the modern and universal values lacking among mass elements may be provided by the institutions of a modern society, for example—education, newspapers, radios, televisions, and travel.[8] These institutions, as represented in the social mobilization index, may indeed have the capacity to foster value systems engendering the communication, cooperation, and understanding conducive to the evolution of a larger socialist community such as the Yugoslav. In summary, then, it is now clear that the set of change stimuli incorporated in the mobilization index suggest value change irrespective of the social-political status of the individual. The primary question involves the apparent inability of the non-elite (i.e., mass) element to be reached by the mobilizing forces. The answer to this question will provide an important key to the rate and scope of individual change in the developing Yugoslav system.

Attitude Change Among Members and Non-Members of the League of Communists

The final control variable divides the sample into those individuals who are members of the Yugoslav League of Communists and those who are not members. The reader is reminded that it was noted earlier in the chapter that party members are more likely to be exposed to the mobilization stimuli than are non-members. It was also noted that due to their general isolation from information stimuli, the non-member group represents a less modern and universalistic sector of the society than does the party member element.[9] The data show, for example, that those belonging to the Yugoslav League of Communists invariably show higher levels of modernism and universalism when compared to the non-member sector. However, such differences yield information solely about the present configurations of values characterizing the two sectors and nothing about the propensity to change. Perhaps a consideration of the three variable model will show a higher correlation between the agents of mobilization and modernized-universalistic value sets among the non-member group. This would suggest that the relatively higher rates of modernism and universalism among the Communist party sector could be accounted for on the basis of their greater access to the mobilization stimuli.

In that respect, a comparison of the change dynamics in each group shows that the overall propensity for change is in fact somewhat higher among the non-member group (see Table 22). The strong coefficient (.48) generated for the mobilization-modernism linkage among the non-member sector indicates that modernized values are highly correlated with exposure to the mobilizing influences.[10] In other words, if a non-member has little or no exposure to the education, mass media, and travel pheonomena, he is unlikely to possess modern beliefs. However, with increases in his level of exposure, his values tend to become modern at a more than significant rate.

TABLE 22

COEFFICIENTS SUMMARIZING RELATIONSHIPS FOR
COMMUNIST PARTY MEMBERSHIP GROUPS

COMMUNIST PARTY MEMBERSHIP GROUPS	Three Relationships		
	Mobilization-Modernism $(A \rightarrow B)$	Mobilization-Universalism $(B \rightarrow C)$	Mobilization-Universalism $(A \rightarrow C)$
Group I: Party Members	.51	.42	.21
Group II: Non-Members	.48	.52	.40

The modernism-universalism (i.e., B-C) linkages within both groups indicate the same relative rate of co-variation as the A-B linkages (see Table 22). Namely, if a modern value set can be effected among both sectors of the sample, the propensity for universalistic orientations follows at a significant and relatively similar rate. However, the value change represented in the mobilization-universalism (i.e., A-C) linkage among the non-member group shows a significantly larger increase in the relative level of universalism with increases in the level of mobilization. This indicates that Communist party members are more likely to be universalistic irrespective of levels of mobilization, while contrastingly, mobilization tends to be a necessary prerequisite or condition for a universalistic set of values among the non-party element. In general, it should be noted that although both groups illustrate extremely strong linkages between all combinations of variables, the general pattern among the non-member group implies that their low modernism and universalism rates can be substantially reduced by exposing members of this sector to increasing levels of the mobilization stimuli.

The findings drawn from this section suggest that the more traditional and particularistic value configurations of the non-member element can be traced to their general isolation from the mobilization stimuli. The findings suggest further that if mobilization could be increased among this more isolated sector, changes toward more modern and more universal belief systems may result. Furthermore, the strength of the coefficients presented in Table 22 imply that the change may even be greater among non-member than among the more modern members of the party.[11]

The above analysis has shown that mobilization is still a scarce resource and varies in distribution among the Yugoslav populace. And although education levels, exposure to the mass media, and internal and external travel rates are climbing yearly on the aggregate level, there are still sizable sectors of the society who remained unreached. This general isolation from the change stimuli suggests a differential rate of value change within the system.

The author noted earlier that the mobilization resource was more likely to be found in the more highly developed republics and within more developed communes within each of the republics. Now, when moving the level of analysis from the political unit to various sectors within the overall society, the data show that the change stimuli are more likely to be found among some groups than others. First, the distribution of mobilization showed a slight curvilinear pattern among groups defined on the basis of age. Older sectors of the society were found to be the least "mobilized," the middle age sector was the most "mobilized," and the youngest sector displayed an intermediate level. Then, when moving to groups defined according to social-political status, extreme differences were found. The higher status social, cultural, and political groups, as well as the party member sector exhibited considerably higher levels of mobilization than did the lower status, rank and file masses. Not surprisingly, the elite sectors were found to possess belief systems that were considerably more modern and universalistic than those characterizing the mass sector.

However, a consideration of the change phenomena within each of the control groups showed that value change was just as likely among the masses and non-party elements once mobilization was attained. The correlation between the mobilization stimuli and modernized values was strong, as well as between that set of values and levels of universalism. The findings suggest that value systems among the masses will tend to become more modernized and universalistic if they can be reached by greater levels of mobilization stimuli. The same is true among elite sectors as already evidenced by their more modern and universal value systems.

It might be noted in conclusion that Yugoslavia's attempts over the long run to build a modern, integrated political community are likely to be successful to the extent that all sectors within the society develop value systems engendering such a political form. Through the use of survey research, this investigation has identified a critical shortcoming in their developmental process. In short, two crucial differences have been found between two important sectors of the society. One sector, composed primarily of elites, has access to a valuable developmental resource: the impetus for value change. However, the data have shown that, to a large extent, the rank and file masses are being "missed" by the mobilization forces. The majority of this sector are still unlikely to have attained a high education and all of the modernizing skills that it implies. Furthermore, they exhibit lower rates of mass media utilization and, therefore, possess lower information levels. Lastly, they are unlikely to possess the resources necessary to travel widely, and hence, do not enjoy the cultural contact that such travel implies. As a result, this sector of Yugoslav society is more likely to be isolated from the outside world and less likely to be equipped with those resources fostering a modern, universalistic value system. In all fairness to the Yugoslav leadership, it should perhaps be noted that the gap between elites and masses is not an intentional result of Yugoslav policy. A consideration of their efforts show that their decision-makers have gone to considerable lengths to mobilize the masses. They have established and encouraged adult and workers' education centers, organized workers' travel programs, and ensured the wide and free flow of information, Still, as in all developing countries, a certain and perhaps inevitable gap exists. However, Yugoslavia's ability to resolve this problem represents an important factor likely to determine the growth of a modernized and integrated socialist community among the traditionally isolated sectors of its population.

CHAPTER VII

UNIVERSALISTIC ATTITUDES
AND A REVIVAL OF NATIONALISM

A. Introduction

As noted at the outset of this study, Yugoslavia in the early 1970's was caught in the throes of a "nationalist revival." Competition between certain nations within the federation had developed into a volatile struggle and, at least on the surface, it appeared that inter-ethnic feelings and tolerance had taken a change for the worse. In view of the developments, various observers, both within and outside of Yugoslavia, agreed that the fragile fabric of the federation was being stretched to the danger point. Finally, Tito and his supporters decided to move quickly and dramatically to preserve the political union, a move which met with both support and disdain.

In view of this reputed escalation in nationalist sentiment, it would seem instructive to examine more fully the nature of inter-ethnic attitudes during the middle and late 1960's. Did other surveys asking other questions, for example, give any indication of the national-based conflict that was to ensue? What we need to know at this juncture is more about the structure of individual and group attitudes in the 1960's, and furthermore, about their relationship to the national situation of the early 1970's.

B. Additional Attitude Surveys

In 1964, the Center for Public Opinion Research in Belgrade ran a survey asking respondents whether they thought relations among the nationalities were good, satisfactory, or bad. On the basis of the interviews, 81% of the 2700 individuals surveyed considered national relations to be "good" or "satisfactory" (See Table 23)[1] On the basis of this broad, sweeping overview of the Yugoslav populace, we would seem to have had little basis for predicting the subsequent national crisis.

When classifying the broader sample by nationality and republic (as in Table 23), the picture seems to be the same. For example, the responses of the Serbs and Croats give little hint of the impending "separatist" or "unitarist" movements. Among members of the Croat nationality, 79.1%

TABLE 23

INTER-ETHNIC RELATIONS IN YUGOSLAVIA, 1964

Percentage of Respondents Believing
Relations Good or Satisfactory

By Nationality	%	By Republic or Province	%
Magyars	93.2	Macedonia	88.8
Macedonians	88.6	Bosnia-Hercegovina	86.7
Moslems	86.7	Vojvodina	82.8
Albanians	80.5	Croatia	82.6
Croats	79.1	Montenegro	78.1
Montenegrins	78.9	Kosovo	78.0
Slovenes	78.9	Serbia (proper)	76.8
Serbs	77.7	Slovenia	75.3
Yugoslav Ave.	81.0	Yugoslav Ave.	81.0

SOURCES: Data compiled from Sergije Pegan, "Opinions on Relations Between Nations in Yugoslavia," in Firdus Dzinić, ed., *Yugoslav Public Opinion Concerning Current Political and Social Questions*, (Belgrade: Institute of Social Sciences, 1964) translated by Joint Publications Research Service (Washington, D.C.), 1970; table adapted from R. V. Burks, *The National Problem and the Future of Yugoslavia*, (Santa Monica, Calif.: The Rand Corporation, October 1971), p. 43.

considered national relations to be either "good" or "satisfactory." In respect to the Serbian nationality, 77.7% viewed national relations in the same favorable fashion. Even though the Serbs and Croats did not view national relations as positively as some other groups (e.g., the Magyars and Macedonians), their overall response could in no way be viewed as providing reason for pessimism concerning the future of national relations. Overall, few would have used these responses to forecast the impending revival of nationalism, particularly on the basis of the figures in which 81% of the total population, and no less than 77% of any one national group, viewed national relations in a positive frame.

But perhaps these data were not really indicative of national feelings in the country. Perhaps it was easier and more expedient for an individual to say that relations were good, while in fact remaining highly ethnocentric in outlook and behavior. Data gathered during 1966 in another study of ethnic relations confronted the issue of national relations more directly. In this country-wide survey of 2600 respondents, the focus was upon the type of relationship (e.g., marriage, friendship, etc.) the respondent would be willing to accept with respect to members of other nationalities.[2] Using the "Bogardus scale" approach, the survey was used to determine the amount of "ethnic distance" that members of each national or ethnic group would be willing to accept with regard to each of the six specified relationships (e.g., marriage, friendship, etc.)[3] Of the overall sample, nearly 60 per cent exhibited no ethnic distance whatsoever. Furthermore, 80.4% of the 2600 respondents indicated "very slight" or "negligible" ethnic distance (See Table 24). While the Slovenes stand out as the least tolerant of the eight specified groups, the often thought of "problem nationalities"—the Serbs and Croats—show negligible ethnic distance. The overall pattern

TABLE 24

ETHNIC DISTANCE IN YUGOSLAVIA, 1966

Percentage of Respondents Manifesting Very Slight or Negligible Ethnic Distance[a]

By Nationality	%	By Republic or Province	%
Magyars	95.0	Vojvodina	93.5
Albanians	94.6	Bosnia-Hercegovina	85.2
Moslems	89.4	Croatia	83.1
Croats	85.3	Macedonia	81.2
Serbs	81.7	Serbia (proper)	78.9
Montenegrins	78.6	Kosovo	77.0
Macedonians	78.3	Montenegro	75.4
Slovenes	55.2	Slovenia	55.6
Yugoslav Ave.	80.4	Yugoslav Ave.	80.4

[a]These two categories comprise all respondents who answered 34 of the total 42 questions (seven nationalities x six relationships) positively.

SOURCES: Data compiled from Dragomir Pantić, *Ethnic Distance in Yugoslavia*, (Belgrade: Institute of Social Sciences, 1967), translated by Joint Publications Research Service, 1970, pp. 12, 15-16; table adapted from Burks, *op. cit.*, p. 43.

show surprisingly high levels of ethnic tolerance among the various groups and, once again exhibits little portent of the nationalist revival that was to ensue. Generally speaking, then, the attitude surveys of the middle 1960's painted an optimistic picture concerning the future of national relations in Yugoslavia. The attitudinal preconditions to greater cooperation and understanding seemed to be established, and sufficient evidence existed to merit discussion of the evolution of a genuine community of Yugoslav peoples.

Overall then, the attitudinal configurations reflected in all of the available surveys reinforces the optimistic picture painted by our early analysis of attitude change. On the basis of the surveys, there was more than sufficient evidence for suggesting that the attitudes and values underlying national relations were not only good, but growing better.

On the basis of the contradiction that this analysis has confronted—that is, universalistic attitudes and ensuing national crisis—that conclusion must be called into question. Namely, if the attitudes of the 1960's exhibited inter-ethnic understanding and tolerance, and if projections into the future suggested even higher levels of tolerance (universalism) in the years to come, how do we explain the revival of nationalism and subsequent national crisis which followed in the early 1970's?

C. Contemporary Nationalisms: Problems, Fears, and Frustrations

In approaching this complex question, it is necessary to take a position concerning the effect of mass attitudes on the national situation in Yugoslavia. Can we contend, for example, that the revival of nationalism and the resultant tensions among nationalities were tied to the attitudes of the broader society? Specifically, were the Yugoslav groups unable to overcome their past differences and historical animosities, and did this fact result in the tensions of the early 1970's? On the basis of the attitudinal data gathered during the 1960's, and on the basis of my understanding of the situation, the broader Yugoslav populace should not be held fully responsible. That is, the national attitudes present at the escalation of the nationalist crisis were not of the character or intensity to have led to the subsequent unrest. On the contrary, I would argue that the escalation of nationalism was primarily an elitist movement. This movement was led by certain members of the LCY and intelligentsia, and was built and later capitalized upon deep-seated frustrations within the Yugoslav populace. Not surprisingly, therefore, the surveys of attitudes concerning national relations provided little insight into the events that were to come.

In my estimation, then, the escalation in nationalist sentiment among the broader populace in the late 1960's was more of a consequence than a cause. Specifically, the nationalist sentiment appeared to result from the following set of circumstances. Due to unresolved problems of an economic, political, and cultural nature in Yugoslavia, fairly widespread frustration characterized the populace. Although initially latent, this frustration was seized upon by certain political and cultural leaders and explained, and sometimes accounted for, in national terms. After the elites opened this release-mechanism for the venting of individual and mass frustration, certain sectors of the populace began to "rationalize" their frustrations in this manner. Then, what started as an elite movement began to take on a mass character.

To an increasing degree, national symbols and sentiments became vehicles which were used and played upon by various leaders and intellectuals in some of the constituent republics to explain the difficulties—and perhaps at times, to rationalize their own shortcomings—incurred in the Yugoslav developmental process. Well-intentioned leaders, such as the now replaced Miko Tripalo and Savka Dabčević-Kučar, capitalized (sometimes inadvertently and other times intentionally) on the underlying fears and insecurities of the Croatian populace by accounting for developmental shortcomings in national terms. Even more significant perhaps were the overtly national appeals and explanations made by such Croatian scholars as Sime Djodan and Marko Veselica. They explained Croatian problems as directly resultant of the Croatian republic's unfavorable and exploited situation in the Yugoslav federation. Similar personalities and appeals were evidenced in other republics. In carrying on what was really an ideological struggle under the guise of nationalism, they exploited mass frustrations and attempted to account for them—or perhaps more accurately, their causes—in national terms. This gave rise to a new form of particularism, and subsequently, defined the setting in which a crisis in national relations developed.

Of course, the ease with which frustrations were converted into nationalism among the populace forces us to critically re-examine the national attitudes of the 1960's. It would not seem unreasonable to argue that the favorable attitudes surveyed at that time were only opinions, and that the underlying animosities were never completely broken down and dissolved. In other words, although favorable attitudes may have existed, the basic value or belief structures of the populace still contained a considerable degree of ethnocentrism of one sort or another. Then, when certain elites begin to play upon various national themes in what was to become a crisis-type setting, national sentiments among the populace were once again brought to the surface.

In order to understand this setting and the ease with which frustrations were transposed into and rationalized through nationalism, it is necessary to look at the basic problems confronting the Yugoslav federation. Indeed, the nature of these problems is such that they lend themselves to an interpretation that can be easily tied to the question of nationality and, therefore, could be transposed into national terms without great difficulty. What were these problems, how might they lead to frustrations, and how might these frustrations be rationalized in national terms?

The initial problem confronting Yugoslavia is of an economic nature and includes all of the difficulties and shortcomings surrounding the Yugoslav economic model. As is widely known, one of the most sensitive questions on the Yugoslav economic scene is that of regional economic development, and the role that the individual republics and federation should play in effecting its achievement. The problem of economics in Yugoslavia, and all of the attendant fears and insecurities it implies, is a source of frustration and conflict expressing a very fundamental relationship to the national question. The basic point of controversy concerns the relative contribution that each of the national republics and provinces should make to the overall development of the federation. As one might expect, the more developed northern republics (Croatia, Slovenia) feel they are carrying more than their fair share of the burden in the federation's attempt to develop the more southern regions. Consequently, socio-economic shortcomings in the more developed republics are often attributed to their "exploited" position.[4] Overall, the problem is of a multi-faceted nature and includes such additional but related issues and controversies as foreign currency exchange, credit policy, investments, and so forth. Taken together, the issues combine to create a problem which the leaders of the various republics have used to launch a fierce ideological struggle, a struggle that is often disguised under the mantle of nationalism in order to rationalize and justify shortcomings in their own policies and performance.

The second problem is of a political nature and reflects the relative power and influence that each of the national units possesses in the Yugoslav federation. The basic issue is whether there should be a party monopoly with power concentrated in the federal center or, on the other hand, greater political decentralization within a genuine self-managing system. The dilemma confronting Yugoslavia is that it has so far found the problem insoluble. While preaching decentralization and firmly believing in the benefits and superiority of power dispersion and the self-management system, the party has been unwilling to relinquish ultimate power. What evolves is a high level of ambiguity and uncertainty regarding power distributions within the Yugoslav federation.

Additional questions relating to the larger political problem mentioned above concern such sensitive issues as the location of the federal capital in Serbia and the over-representation of Serbian bureaucrats which that location necessitates. Also involved is the question of succession and the basic uncertainties surrounding the performance of the Collective State Presidency upon the passing of Tito. These and other political-based questions have resulted in frustrations among both elites and masses. Even a cursory reading of the newspapers and journals coming from the republics and provinces during the late 1960's and early 1970's makes that fact abundantly clear.[5] In one way or another, every national group finds some "injustice" with which to be concerned. While the Croats dislike the capital's placement in Belgrade, the Serbs tire of constant complaining on the part of the Croats. Sooner or later, the perceptions of political "injustice" take on a nationalist tone.

The final problem area leading to expressions of nationalism in Yugoslavia concerns the cultural and social status of various groups and individuals. Although the Yugoslav government has made considerable progress by guaranteeing the equality and rights of the various national groups, guarantees that have led to a practical institutionalization far exceeding that of most other multi-national states, certain insecurities still exist. The less populous nationalities and ethnic groups fear the power capabilities of the larger. The larger, on the other hand, fear the future effects of population booms among the smaller. The Croats perceive the assimilatory potential of the Serbian language and culture, and undertake measures to establish their distinctness and own identity.[6] The Albanians of Kosovo become disturbed about their provincial status, their less privileged level of social conditions, and their less developed sense of cultural identity. Additional examples of status difficulties and insecurities abound.

Taken together, these three problem areas bring together a host of difficulties which confront the Yugoslav peoples. Over the last five years, these difficulties became increasingly discussed—both within the party, and within certain intellectual and scholarly circles—from the point of nationality. Elites of various backgrounds used national-based explanations of one sort or another to account for the frustrations emanating within their constituencies, and furthermore, to direct criticism away from the shortcomings and failures of their own policies. Nationalism, in turn, became the vehicle by which these frustrations and justifications were often expressed.

D. Relative Deprivation:
The Root of Frustrations and Nationalisms

Within post-war Yugoslavia, the ideology of the new Marxist state created high expectations among both leaders and followers. Economic development and material abundance was to be accomplished both easily and rapidly. The impressive gains subsequently made during the fifties and sixties raised Yugoslav expectations even higher. Political relationships and former power inequalities were to be resolved through the self-management sytem and through regional decentralization. Finally, the new ideology ensured a community of peoples with equal rights and status. In theory, at least, the Communist system resolved to end the cultural and social injustices of the old.

Given the initial success of the revolutionary movement and the postwar legitimacy and popularity the Titoist state commanded, a good part of the ideology was internalized or "taken to heart." Through the 1960's, national attachments softened as the ideology had predicted. In some cases, it appeared to produce an end to the former economic, political, and cultural difficulties. However, when the problems subsequently persisted, frustrations resulted which had a propensity to open the individual to nationalist forces. These forces had the effect of leading the individual back to his more traditional and particularistic attachments—i.e., his nation, religion, and cultural heritage.

Stipe Šuvar, high ranking member of the Croatian League of Communists, sociology professor at Zagreb University, and an outspoken critic of nationalism, describes the resultant situation as follows:

> After having been drunk on ideology, which was destroying everything that was old and which promised the rapid creation of happiness on earth; after having become disappointed by the results of such a radical ideology, people have started sobering up and trying to return to the old, lost values: the religious and ethnic communities.[7]

Šuvar goes on to argue that when individuals lose their perspective for progress, and become frustrated by their social problems, they seek refuge in their ethnic group, which is reflected in ethnocentrism and hatred directed toward other nationalities. In my estimation, Šuvar would have been more accurate if he were to have noted that the "sobering process" established a socio-psychological setting with a definite propensity for the development of nationalist sentiment. This propensity was subsequently activated when certain elements of the leadership capitalized upon and rationalized the existing frustrations for personal and political gain.

Before proceeding with the argument, however, we should make the following inquiries. Why did frustrations develop, and why did they result in nationalism? In my opinion, the basic factor leading to high levels of individual and mass frustration in Yugoslavia can be viewed as the discrepancy between what Yugoslav individuals and groups thought they deserved, and what they felt capable of attaining. Put in the terminology of relative deprivation theory, frustration resulted from the discrepancy between value expectations and value capabilities. While the ideology of the society assured economic growth, political equlibrium, and cultural and social equality—and in so doing, inevitably raised the expectations of the populace—the realities of the situation suggested persistent and recurrent problems. Due to difficulties on the economic scene, for example, and in the self-management system, as well as in regard to the question of cultural status and justice, the individual increasingly viewed the values which he deemed important (i.e., economic security, political power, and social justice) as unattainable. Therefore, while his expectations were high and generally rising due to the ideological exhortations of the state, his perception of the capabilities for realizing such values decreased as the persistent and seemingly insoluble problems remained. If the regime had not promised so much, the disparate gap between expectations and capabilities might never have risen so high. If the ideology had not been used so successfully in raising expectations, the levels of societal discontent might have never escalated. As Runciman puts it, "if people have no reason to expect or hope for more than they can achieve, they will be less discontented with what they have, or even be grateful simply to be able to hold on to it."[8]

The general mood expressed in 1970 and 1971 throughout the newspapers, journals, and other media suggested that Yugoslavia had produced few who were grateful. On the contrary, there were many who expected far more than they were realistically going to receive. When coming to grips with the discrepancy between what they expected and what they received, they felt deprived. This feeling of relative deprivation resulted in frustration and, in the words of Branko Horvat, nationalism became the rationalization of frustration.[9] At this point, the formerly latent nationalist sentiments hidden beneath the seemingly favorable attitudes surveyed in the sixties came back into play. Once again, nationalism became a dominant theme in Yugoslav politics.

In order to understand the idea of relative deprivation more fully, it might be instructive to apply it to two of the variants of nationalism purported to exist in the Yugoslav context. Although we will use the Croatian example to describe the "separatist" variant and the Serbian to describe the "unitarist," it would be unfair to assume that these two nations alone reflect such tendencies. To the contrary, the ideas might be equally applicable in the cases of other national groups.[10]

E. Relative Deprivation and Separatism: The Croatian Example

To some other national groups in Eastern Europe, or even in Yugoslavia for that matter, the Croats' achievement over the post-war years would be gratifying and over and above what might be deemed acceptable. To the average Croatian, however, whose expectations may have been raised to unrealistic and unattainable levels by the promises of certain leaders, by his foreign travels and what he has seen abroad, and by his assessment of Croatia's inherent capabilities (however accurate they may be), the achievements were quite low and often unacceptable. Consequently, his perception of the relatively low level of Croatian success became a source of frustration and discontent. While his expectations of what Croats deserved were high, his perceptions of Croat capabilities *within the Yugoslav federation* were low. The inevitable consequence was the development of individual and group frustration, frustrations which national leaders such as Tripalo and Dabčević-Kučar reflected, and out of which developed the crisis in national relations.

The socio-political dynamics of the Croatian situation can be explained in terms of relative deprivation theory and illustrated in diagram form (see Figure 17). Charted on the vertical axis are those values most relevant to

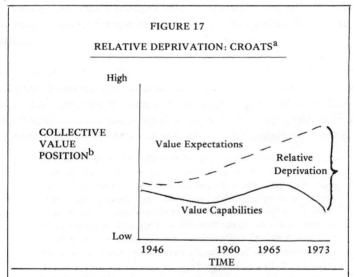

FIGURE 17

RELATIVE DEPRIVATION: CROATS[a]

[a]It should be emphasized that although this diagram is devoid of numbers, it is not without empirical justification. Overall, it reflects a simplified diagram—based upon my research—of Croatian expectations, Croatian perceptions of national capabilities, and how both have changed over time. The same applies to the diagram to follow.

[b]The Collective Value Position refers to those economic, political, and status values which Croats deem important and for which the average Croat strives.

the members of the Croat nationality and to the Yugoslav populace in general. In my estimation, these values correspond with the three problem areas discussed above.[11] Therefore, when we refer to the collective value position, we mean those economic, political, and status conditions deemed important by both elites and masses within the broader society.[12] Accordingly, the designation of Croat *value expectations* refers to the average economic, political and status values to which Croats believe they are justifiably entitled. As illustrated by the broken line in the diagram, this average expectation varies over time and is used to reflect the general rise in Croat hopes and aspirations.

The concept of value expectations refers to the Croatian sense of what is rightfully owed to them as a collective national group. The sense of Croatian "expectation" results from a variety of factors, including what they perceive history has ascribed to them, their position in relation to other nationalities in the federation, and from what their leaders have promised. Taken together, the Croat sense of rightness represents a composite indicator of what they expect within the Yugoslav federation. As noted in the diagram, Croatian expectations have grown progressively over the years. Furthermore, the year 1973 found the Croats expecting substantially more than they perceived themselves capable of attaining.

This leads us to the concept of *value capabilities*, which refers to the amount of the economic, political, and status values members of the Croat nationality perceive themselves able to achieve. Šuvar notes that while Croat nationalists feel that all of these basic values are extremely important to the Croat nation, they are being impeded in the present federation:

> ... the Croatian nation is *economically exploited* in the new Yugoslavia even more than it was in old Yugoslavia, and up until now pronounced Serbian pressure on Croatian *culture* has been manifest; there is Serbian penetration into Croatian ethnic territory and *political domination* of Serbs not only in Yugoslavia as a whole but also in the Republic of Croatia; because of the repression of its *national being* and the difficult *economic position* into which it has been brought, the Croatian people today is displaced and multiplies slowly.[13]
>
> *(emphasis mine)*

It could be contended that such feelings among the Croat "nationalists," along with the widespread frustration evidenced among members of the Croat nationality, can be viewed and explained according to the theory of relative deprivation. Specifically, Croat frustrations resulted from their perception of the discrepancy between their rather high expectations and relatively lower capabilities. While the Croats expected to attain economic levels comparable to West European nations, they perceived their capabilities being impeded within the Yugoslav federation.

Although such ideological exhortations and normal national aspirations caused Croat expectations to grow steadily over the post-war years, a rise in perceived capabilities was more problematical (see Figure 19). Specifically, the capabilities curve (solid line in the diagram) is intended to show that the policy of "Yugoslavism" brought a general decrease in perceptions of Croat capabilities through the early 1960's. After reaching a low around that period, perceptions of capabilities began to rise as a result of the Croats' awareness of the potential effects of movements toward regional decentralization and the economic reforms of 1965. Perceptions of Croat capabilities continued to rise and reached the apex at the time of the far-reaching set of constituional amendments made in the summer of 1971. Had the discrepancy between expectations and capabilities continued to close, the nationalist sentiment among the Croats might eventually have ceased. However, the constitutional amendments of 1971 brought even higher expectations among the Croatians, while the subsequent December replacement of the Croatian leadership brought a sharp down-swing in perceptions of capabilities. The result of this suddenly expanding gap was the open expression of hostility among many Croatian leaders, members of the intelligentsia, and even rank and file citizens.[14]

No better example of this perceived discrepancy and the resulting frustration among the Croats can be given than that expressed in the work of the Croatian economist Sime Djodan. In a variety of articles, Djodan outlines the benefits to which he believes the Croats are justifiably entitled, and then laments that the federation has created obstacles that impede their capabilities for achievement. He compares the Croatian economic situation to that of Norway and other small European countries and contends that Croatian development should and would compare with these more developed countries if it were not for its exploited position within the federal republic. Djodan argues:

> In the opinion of the Swedish economist Gunnar Myrdal, smaller countries like Sweden, Norway, and Denmark have achieved optimal economic power, and if they were lumped into some great agglomeration, they would lose more than benefit. . . . Therefore, the fable now being spread that Croatia will fare badly in the new federation because she has no raw materials, is without any foundation in reality. Croatia has been living for one hundred years solely from her own income and a huge part of her capital accumulation had been drained out without equivalent return. When this unreciprocated drain stops, she can only fare better—considerably better.[15]

Later, Djodan contends that if the constitutional amendments result in changes in the "exploitative" nature of the federation, Croatia's future will be brighter:

> If the financial power of our republic is brought up to the
> level of her productive strength, and if the announced changes
> are carried out in a really consequential and consistent manner,
> very beautiful vistas will open up for the further normal devel-
> opment of Croatia in many areas . . . . But in order for Croatia to
> develop normally, it is necessary that very radical changes be car-
> ried out in the economic system of the SFRY.[16]

Over and over again, Djodan's analysis expresses high expectations regarding Croatian development, and at the same time, low capabilities
resulting from the present federation—"This blocked the development of
Croatia," he notes time after time.[17] And while the bulk of Djodan's work
concerns economic values, the writings and public expressions of others
express similar perceptions of deprivation concerning political and status
values.

Although it should be clearly emphasized that Djodan was not in any
sense a spokesman for the collective will of the Croat people, it is safe to
say that he did reflect some of the sentiments that existed among some
important sectors of the nation. Although more soft-spoken and less ideo-
logically offensive, the public expressions of the now replaced Croatian
party leaders, Tripalo and Dabčević-Kučar, expressed similar if not almost
identical points of view. The important point for this analysis is that the
views expressed publicly by the Croatian party leaders, certain sectors of
the intelligentsia, and various social and cultural elites began to appeal to
the national pride of the Croatian population. What began as an elite expression of dissatisfaction with the federal arrangement and perceived
shortcomings of the SFRY was broadened to include a good part of the
mass population. This is why the attitude surveys cited above reflected
little indication of the national movement that was to ensue. Such feelings
had not yet developed and they did not develop until certain leadership
elements seized upon the deeper seated economic, political, and status
frustrations and began to explain and account for them in national terms.
And since the elite expressions seemed to explain some of the mass's own
difficulties, they began to accept and use the national-based explanations
as a release mechanism to vent their own frustrations. Rather than blaming
one's economic difficulties on oneself, it was much easier to blame them
on the "centralists" in Belgrade. This behavior was practiced among both
elites and masses. The degree to which the national pronouncements and
speeches of the leaders were absorbed and internalized by the mass sectors
determined the extent to which the struggle could turn into a broadly
based national movement. When viewing the Croatian developments of
1971, it appeared that the mass appeal was quite broad indeed.

F. Relative Deprivation and Unitarism: The Serbian Example

It would be unfair and mistaken to assume that all frustrations resided among members of the Croat nationality. To the contrary, the shortcomings and difficulties experienced in Yugoslavia, and giving root to frustrations, have not been limited to one or even a few groups. Therefore, it should be emphasized that frustrations and the resultant national sentiments of one sort or another were to be found among all national groups.[18] It can be noted, in that regard, that certain sectors of the Serb nationality also perceived obstacles to the values they consider important and to which they feel justifiably entitled. Former hopes and expectations surrounding the notion of a "Greater Serbia," or for a more powerful Serbian role in the federation, for example, had not been forsaken among all members of the nationality. Within the SFRY, those who cling to such aspirations find their expectations blocked; opportunities for a "Greater Serbian" state and all of the values it implies, for example, are minimal within the present Yugoslav federation. Among some sectors of the Serbian nation, therefore, the perceived discrepancy between high expectations and low capabilities created a feeling of deprivation. This sense of injustice to the Serbs resulted in a form of frustration which gave rise to the "unitarist" brand of nationalism.

The mention of "unitarism," as compared with the earlier cited "separatism" draws attention to the varieties of nationalism that can arise in a multi-ethnic state. The assumption that Croatian frustrations tend to result in "separatist" feeelings, while Serbian result in "unitarist" is a simplification but not without empirical basis or explanatory merit. The rationalization of frustrations has to be taken in context with the historical and environmental realities of the multi-national condition. Since Croatian perceptions are based upon an awareness of interwar Serbian domination and present Serbian power, Croats consider themselves in a disadvantaged position. Therefore, Croat frustrations and self-interests are rationalized in terms of separatism. The same historical and environmental conditions tend to lead the Serbs to a "unitaristic" (implying unity and centralism) approach. The Serbian rationalization of frustration is based upon the assumption that Serbian values could be more readily served through increased "unity," dominated, of course, by the Serbian power center in Belgrade.

When looking for the roots of "unitarism" in Serbia, it may be useful to turn once again to the ideas of relative deprivation. In following the rise in expectations among the Serbian nationality, we can assume that expectations were always high within the Yugoslav federation and generally climbed over the years (see Figure 18). The reasons for the rising expectations

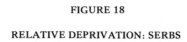

FIGURE 18

RELATIVE DEPRIVATION: SERBS

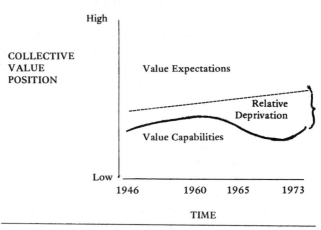

were numerous and involved the history of an independent state tradition, the position of dominance in interwar Yugoslavia, the numerical strength of the nationality, and so on. Perceptions of value capabilities in the Yugoslav federation, on the other hand, have been somewhat problematic and are likely to be based upon and vary with changes in Yugoslav nationalities policy. Generally speaking, the earlier "Yugoslavism" and centralist approach led to a rise in perceptions of national value capabilities among members of the Serbian group. This general increase is illustrated by the line of rising capabilities in the diagram (see Figure 18). However, after the steady increase through the 1950's and 60's, a decline in perceived capabilities was experienced as the former policy came under increasing criticism and was finally discredited (see the decline indicated between 1960 and 1965 in Figure 18). Finally, Serbian perceptions of value capabilities reached a post-war low with the adoption of the constitutional amendments of 1971, which took even greater power from the federal government in Belgrade. However, with the recent recentralization and reassertion of Party control which followed the nationalist outbreak of 1971, Serbian capabilities evidence a marked up-swing. At the same time, the level of discrepancy between expectations and capabilties is still generally high and, therefore, can be expected to lead to continued feelings of deprivation and its consequence, mass and individual frustration.

Suvar defines the outgrowth of such frustration in terms of the following Serbian perceptions:

> The Serbian people is injured and abused in the new Yugoslavia although it contributed most to its creation and is the most important force for its preservation; sins which are either mutual or the fruit of a conspiracy of members of other nationalities are blamed on the Serbian people; Croatian nationalism is engaged in a striking assault, and among the Croatian nation subversive and ruffian forces are again on the scene, threatening even the existence of Yugoslavia and the Serbian people, which has outgrown nationalism and is characterized by general internationalism.[19]

Therefore, while the Serbian people had high and generally rising expectations within the new Yugoslavia, they perceived difficulties and obstacles impeding their attainment. Many of these difficulties were attributed to the "subversive assaults" of other groups, nationalist assaults which were perceived as having worked to lower Serbian opportunities to achieve the economic, political, and status conditions to which they felt entitled. This discrepancy resulted in a sense of relative deprivation within the Yugoslav context which, in turn, led to a sense of individual and mass frustration within the Serbian populace. This frustration provided the basis for a "unitarist" movement, a movement which rationalized Serbian difficulties as the consequence of the decentralized, fragmented state.

As evidenced by the recent assault on all forms of Yugoslav nationalism, "unitarism" proved to be no "sacred cow." When the central party leadership removed the Croatian nationalists from power in 1971 and restructured the Croatian party leadership, the "unitarists" temporarily saw themselves as the victors. Shortly thereafter, however, the Party declared that the "unitarists" were equally as dangerous as the "separatists." The new Secretary of the Executive Committee of the Serbian Central Committee notes: "One of the difficulties in the struggle against Greater Serbian nationalism has been the fact that in Serbia unitarism has never been considered as nationalism."[20] Now that it is, the war on nationalism of all shades and colors continues.

G. Possible Alternatives

When the Communists came to power in post-war Yugoslavia, they hoped to tranform a fragmented, cleavage-ridden society into a genuine socialist community based upon the ideals of "brotherhood and unity." The structure of national attitudes indicated by the middle and late 60's seemed to suggest that considerable progress had been made. Almost all individuals contended that national relations were good or satisfactory, and a strong majority showed complete ethnic tolerance on the ethnic distance scale. In addition, analysis of attitude change and projections into the future suggested that attitude systems in Yugoslavia would become even more tolerant and "universalistic" as the post-war years passed. Empirical analysis revealed that as the average Yugoslav became more exposed to information, and more modern in his beliefs, he also became more "universalistic" within the traditionally particularistic Yugoslav setting. During this seemingly serene era of Yugoslav development (1960-70), few foresaw the revival of nationalism that was to come.

In 1971 and 1972, however, the Yugoslav federation was permeated with national-based conflict. The hope for a united socialist community based upon the ideals of brotherhood and unity seemed suddenly imperiled. In view of this development, the cause of the national crisis becomes an important question. The argument set forth in this chapter was that the roots of the crisis could not be found in the national attitudes of the populace, but rather in deeper seated frustrations resulting from unresolved problems within Yugoslav society. As the persistent problems of economics, politics, and culture became more and more perplexing to the regional-based leadership and intelligentsia, they increasingly turned to national-based explanations to account for the difficulties residing in their constituent republics. These explanations, along with the more direct exhortations of certain sectors of the intelligentsia, capitalized upon the frustrations of the broader populace. These circumstances seemed to establish the setting in which nationalism became the means by which to rationalize existing frustration.

Although the Croatian and Serbian cases were singled out for closer attention in order to develop the argument in this chapter, it should not be inferred that the other nationalities are in some way immune to the discussion. The socio-psychological dynamics of perceived deprivation, frustration, and a resulting propensity for nationalism are common to all groups. It might also be added that it is only natural for the nations and ethnic groups of Yugoslavia to see their positions as being potentially threatened within the multi-national union. It can be considered as natural on the basis of facts gathered from the experiences of other multi-national states, experiences which suggest that fears of assimilation and attendant processes are not always unfounded. Under such circumstances, feelings of insecurity and the escalation of nationalist activity develop almost automatically as defenses to one's threatened national interests.

How can such escalations of nationalism be avoided? What strategy might be available to the leaders of Yugoslavia in order to deal with this apparently universal phenomenon? Although the central leadership's response to the national crisis of 1971 might have been advisable and politically expedient in the short run, its long range effect may be more questionable. The effect of the reassertion of Party control and unity seems problematical over the long run because it appears to deal with the consequences and symptoms of nationalism, and in and of itself, directs rather little attention to the causes of such movements.

A reasonable approach, it seems, would be one which attempted to directly confront and deal with the three problem areas of Yugoslav development. This is not to say that the Yugoslav leaders have ignored the basic economic, political, and status questions confronting their peoples, nor is it to say that the overall progress they have made has not been significant. It is to say, however, that imaginative programs should be developed and additional resources allocated to resolving the problems that have led to past frustrations. This renewed effort may have the real effect of raising the capabilities of the Yugoslav state and, in turn, act to raise national perceptions (e.g., Croatian) of their own capabilities within the Yugoslav federation.

At the same time, the Yugoslav leaders should be sensitive to the high expectations that still exist among the national groups and avoid any action that might work to raise them higher. High aspirations can lead to "achieving societies," and a faster pace of social and economic development. Unattainable expectations, on the other hand, can have serious repercussions and be detrimental to optimal state development. Ideally, the regime might attempt to lower such expectations to more modest levels having closer correspondence with social reality. This might be accomplished in the Yugoslav situation if the LCY were to take a position of greater realism and honesty with the people. The regime could caution the populace that the road from the underdeveloped, fragmented Yugoslavia of 1945 to a developed, integrated socialist community of the future is not an easy journey. To the Titoist regime's credit, it should be pointed out that its behavior in this regard has been largely satisfactory. For the most part in recent years, it has been frank with its people and unwilling to ignore the basic challenges in its environment. At the same time, it must resolve to do more in closing the gap between hopes and realities, between what the various Yugoslav peoples think they should receive and what the system is capable of providing. By so doing, the Yugoslav state can work to resolve the difficulties which now confront it, and make further progress in what already appears to be a remarkable journey toward the construction of a genuine community of nations.

CHAPTER VIII

THE INDIVIDUAL IN YUGOSLAVIA: IMPLICATIONS RAISED FOR AN EVOLVING SOCIALIST COMMUNITY

> Governments can modify communities, and they can make communities in rare and favorable situations; but on the whole it is the communities which make governments.
>
> —Karl Deutsch[1]

A. Introduction

Over the long run, the degree of community among the South Slavic peoples will be likely to determine the fate of the Yugoslav state. If the predominant values of certain groups or individuals view their future as brighter outside of the Yugoslav union, secessionist threats may develop. Or, if the values of the representatives of one nation express a desire for and are successful in gaining an excessive share of the power within the federal system, a potentially oppressive, highly centralized system may result. However, if the values of the populace evolve in a manner that represents an increasing acceptance of all individuals and nations as legitimate and equal participants in the Yugoslav union, then the future development of a genuine socialist community may be more likely.

B. The Yugoslav Pattern

This study addressed itself to some probable determinants of the three possibilities raised in the introduction, and concluded that if given sufficient time to develop, the third pattern may not be an unreasonable alternative. Although the events of the early 1970's suggested that the first two possibilities were perhaps more in line with recent experience, they should not be considered as ruling out the possibility for the latter alternative. The human dimension of community development does not necessarily follow a continual linear path, but may manifest breaks, discontinuities, and even reversals. In this respect, the revival of nationalisms during the early seventies might be viewed as a temporary discontinuity in a long-range building process. Corresponding difficulties—even in the form of reversals—have been experienced in the histories of much older multi-ethnic communities. Although breaks and reversals are generated within the development process, the search for a mutually beneficial form of political union goes on.

In order to approach the subject of community-building in a manner that could be disciplined and supported by empirical data, this study concentrated upon the configuration and evolution of a number of determinants of community—that is, a collection of social characteristics and value sets of a country-wide sample of the Yugoslav populace. It was argued at the outset that the Yugoslav's ability to realize the trademarks of a genuine political community—that is, communication, cooperation, and understanding—among the diverse and often conflicting South Slavic peoples was dependent upon a certain collection of characteristics and values of its citizenry. The study posited, for example, that the capacity to read, to travel, and the opportunity to expose oneself to the influences of mass media were important determinants of the behaviors upon which communities were based. It was also contended that the expressed values of the Yugoslav populace could be viewed as important indicators affecting the likelihood of the citizenry to engage in these behaviors. If it has been shown that these individual attributes are more likely to be found among one sector than another, or that a certain dynamic is likely to engender the growth or decline of these attributes, then the study has progressed toward isolating some important phenomena and dynamics in the community-building process, and therefore, has accomplished its main objective.

It is common knowledge that one of the most important tasks facing the post-war leadership element in Yugoslavia was the need to generate a new set of values among the citizenry. The regime had hoped to encourage a pattern of values that would transcend former nationalistic, localistic, and other particularistic barriers, and at the same time, create new loyalties at a higher form of socialist experience. In the conclusion to Shoup's important study, he comments:

> The dilemma of Communism and the national question in Yugoslavia has been one, in a sense, of nation-building: utilizing existing pro-Yugoslav sentiment in support of economic, cultural, and social policies aimed at slowly breaking down national barriers and creating new loyalties. Especially among the younger generation of Yugoslavs it would seem that such policies should have been highly effective.[2]

Although many breaks or difficulties have been experienced since the publication of Shoup's book, the development of new loyalties is undeniable, and further, is likely to continue in future years and among future generations.

Overall, the Yugoslavs' strategy was to follow two basic and fundamentally different sets of rationale. The first was based upon a blending of

Marxist theory and Yugoslav nationality policy, and the second relied upon predictions of modernization logic. On the basis of the first rationale, the Yugoslavs predicted that the class struggle would inevitably and increasingly transcend provincial loyalties, and as the forces of socialist development continued, more particularistic values would invariably fade away. The second line of reasoning argued that the conditions created by increased socio-economic development would engender higher levels of individual mobilization and modernization. These two phenomena, the Yugoslavs contended, would result in the dissolution, or at least softening, of more personal, parochial, and provincial loyalties within the Yugoslav system.

The analysis represented in this study concentrated primarily upon the latter strategy and concluded that the Yugoslavs' developmental logic did in fact receive empirical support. When examining this change sequence in considerable detail, it was found that the transformation of individual characteristics and value systems is taking place in a fairly predictable fashion—namely, the process of individual change shows some important regularities, and furthermore, that these regularities correspond with the sequential, cumulative pattern of change hypothesized at the outset. The data confirmed that with the increases in mobilization brought about by increased social and economic development, the Yugoslav citizen tends to assume more modernized and less particularistic value sets irrespective of nationality, environmental setting, age, socio-political position, or membership in the Yugoslav League of Communists.

The data also indicated, however, that the strength of this developmental relationship deviated from the country-wide pattern in a number of important control groups. That is, the dynamics of the change process varied somewhat depending upon the nature and composition of the population. Among the Slovenes, for example, the effect of increased mobilization upon traditionalism and particularism was much less meaningful than among members of the other national groups. While a certain increase in mobilization brought about substantial increases in modernism and universalism among Macedonians, for example, it had considerably less impact upon Slovenes. It was concluded, however, that mobilization encourages more modern and universalistic value orientations among all sectors of the society and potentially, at least, has the power to engender the communication, cooperation, and understanding conducive to the evolution of a genuine socialist community.

According to scientific canons, it is difficult for one to say that a certain model or theory has been verified or rejected. Such is the case with the model used in this study. At the same time, however, the pattern found in this analysis received empirical support within every sub-group considered in the study. These sub-groups, moreover, represented almost every conceivable sector of Yugoslav society. In short, the pattern has been disciplined and supported by data that permit inferences going considerably beyond speculations often offered in respect to the Yugoslav development process.

It has not been contended that this pattern of mobilization and value change will increase the "happiness quotient" in Yugoslavia, as Lerner suggests it invariably does in the six developing nations he studied, or that it will stabilize the Yugoslav political scene, as some integration theorists might contend.[3] In the Yugoslav case there are simply too many unknowns. However, the fact that this process of change is evident within the country, and further, that it is having clearly identifiable results, is undeniable and important in itself. As people in many different professions told the author during his study in the country, "the people are coming to the cities, changing their perspectives, and won't go back." Perhaps the crucial question that concerns us at this point is not whether change is taking place—and the foregoing chapters have certainly indicated that it is—but rather whether there are problems raised by such change, and if so, the capacity of Yugoslav leaders and policies to deal with certain difficulties they are likely to create.

C. Problems and Strategies

It must be noted in this concluding chapter that the Yugoslavs have found it necessary to adopt certain strategies to counter two over-riding problems incurred during the process of rapid mobilization and value change.[4] One problem resulting from the change process outlined in the previous chapters concerns a developmental consequence incurred by all systems committed to raising the skills and level of modernization of their citizenry. Namely, the regime is finding an increasingly sophisticated citizenry with which it must contend. From the viewpoint of the social or political engineer, the predominantly peasant society of pre-war Yugoslavia was in many respects a less skilled, articulate, and demanding populace and, therefore, a simpler population to manage and control.[5] However, with migration to the cities and ensuing mobilization and modernization, a different citizenry is evolving. The essence of the problem created by an increasingly mobilized and modernized character is pointedly raised in the comments of one developmental theorist concerned with the mobilization phenomenon:

> If, through economic and social planning, one increases the rate
> of popular mobilization, one also increases the demands made on
> the government. Although this mobilization is essential for build-
> ing national sentiment among the masses, it may also threaten the
> regime if the government cannot keep pace with the new demands.[6]

The suggestions are not inappropriate to the case in Yugoslavia. The more mobilized and modernized and, in general, more sophisticated citizenry has not proven to be the docile, more meagerly equipped "followers" found immediately after the War. However, the Yugoslav regime has not been unaware of this change within the citizenry and has instituted an appropriate and perhaps ingenious strategy coming under the general title of *samoupravljanje* (self-government). Inaugurated first as workers' self-management in Yugoslav factories in the early 1950's and subsequently broadened to include almost all conceivable aspects of social, political, and economic life, the self-government movement represents a significant attempt to allow the individual to utilize his developing skills and express his growing desires. This strategy has resulted in one of the most extensive and intricate structures for participatory democracy ever attempted in a complex, developing social system.[7]

In other words, by opening up the channels and encouraging the citizenry to participate, the regime has followed a strategy that helps absorb the demands expressed by an increasingly sophisticated citizenry and, at the same time, helps divert attention from what Lerner calls the "revolution of rising expectation."[8] In its simplest form, the self-government strategy allows the regime to counter demands with the following rationale: if certain expectations and needs have not been met, the citizenry must hold themselves responsible since they have been trained and encouraged to participate and are, therefore, responsible for their own social, political, and economic affairs.

The underlying strategy of the regime in this respect has been to mobilize and modernize the citizenry at the most rapid rate and, by so doing, hope to generate the individual characteristics and value systems most conducive to a dynamic, integrated community. However, since it was important and necessary for the regime to develop institutional structures corresponding with the human concomitants of these rapid changes, it had to devise an appropriate plan providing what might be called a dynamic equilibrium between the developing skills and needs of the changing citizenry. Its two-fold strategy has thus been to pursue the modernization logic in order to provide a certain dynamism to the process and, at the same time, develop the idea of participatory democracy which is carefully presided over by the League of Communists in order to provide a stabilizing measure.

The Yugoslavs' use of the two-fold strategy (i.e., modernization and self-government) and the resulting blend of societal dynamism and societal stability, closely reflects the theorizing of Samuel Huntington. The central thesis of Huntington's *Political Order in Changing Societies* is that optimal development and political order are obtained when organizational growth is compatible with the rate of social mobilization and modernization.[9] He contends that the largest problem confronting the developing system results when mobilized, modernized citizens outgrow the structures capable of meeting their skills, demands, and needs. In effect, the Yugoslavs have addressed themselves to this problem by attempting the synchronization of these forces. They have done so largely by pursuing the strategy outlined above.

Most specifically, they have faced the question of societal equilibrium by attempting to synchronize the dynamics of individual change with the stability provided by the institutions of self-government and party control. Whether or not this synchronization can continue as the change process evolves will provide an important key to the Yugoslav future.

The author has found another extremely important and potentially disruptive problem resulting from the general pattern of value change outlined in the foregoing chapters. This problem concerns the role of a sociocultural sector—specifically, certain social, cultural, and religious elites—which detests some important aspects of the change pattern toward increased universalism. Namely, these articulate and potentially powerful leaders, predominantly drawn from the social and cultural realm although also in some cases from the political, react negatively to any hints of a populace less attached to national symbols and, hence, more conducive to an integrated, homogeneous, and unified federal system. These sectors are sophisticated enough to see the general trend that is evolving. They can not avoid seeing the inroads that the country-wide television network and other media are making upon the values of the society.[10] It is becoming increasingly clear to representatives of these sectors that the effects of twentieth century industrialization and technology are changing value systems and in a manner that is potentially dangerous to the preservation of national and cultural differences.[11] And since these sectors are closely and emotionally tied to the importance of cultural distinctness in the Yugoslav setting, they react negatively and show disdain toward any signs exhibiting a dissolution of ethno-cultural differences.

Perhaps fortunately, the regime has not placed excessive emphasis on "Yugoslav" themes which would further alienate and intensify the feelings of those closely tied to national symbols, as well as run the risk of associating the regime with an "assimilationist" policy. On the contrary, the strategy of the regime in this respect has amounted to a highly appropriate policy of cultural equality and autonomy, although always expressed within the framework of a federal, socialist community of nations. This policy has undergone a number of changes fluctuating between the more centralized "Yugoslavism" orientation which followed the war, to the high level of decentralization and regional autonomy that is expressed at present.[12]

However, when the more culturally motivated and particularistic sectors being discussed in this section view the general, country-wide value trends toward universalism in the country, they find little comfort in the reputed autonomy and equality provided by the regime. In fact, they perceive a further erosion of cultural distinctness that must be met with some strategy or tactics of their own.

However, since the official policy of the regime has always been directed toward the development of an integrated socialist community, and since it has become even more zealous in the aftermath of the 1971-72 crisis, the tactics available to the advocates of cultural identity and distinctiveness are limited and must be kept within certain boundaries. At best, most of their efforts take the form of delaying tactics, or are often pursued in a *sub rosa* manner. The general strategy is to counter any policy and behavior that suggest assimilation of cultural distinctness which, of course, includes nationality, language, and other lower-order elements—namely, those elements cited in the particularism index of the study. It remains outside of this study's objectives, and in fact is impossible and outside of the scope of science, to predict how successful the efforts of these delaying tactics and restraining efforts will be. Recent experience suggests, however, that they can bring certain discontinuities to the development process. The cultural journals in a number of republics were involved intimately in the expression of nationalist sentiment during the late 1960's and early 70's, and encouraged the renewed use of national symbols in social, cultural, and political life. Their intention was to emphasize national themes so they would not be forgotten, but would rather be magnified to show one's own distinctness in the hope of re-establishing a clear sense of national identification. Such organizations were severely treated by the Titoist response and forced to curtail what the government branded as nationalist activities. At the present they represent forces that will have to be reconciled as the process of development continues.

D. Conclusion

Over the long run it will be impossible for the Yugoslavs to "homogenize" their system in the sense that all individuals and nations subscribe to the same values and symbols. It will also be difficult, if not impossible, for the leaders to generate a system of values that will be based upon the total equality and acceptance of all sectors in the society. However, it may not be impossible for the individual Yugoslav to learn something more about his neighbor, his culture, his needs, and desires. Accordingly, it may become increasingly possible for this individual to detach himself from the more personal and provincial values of his own existence without losing sight of his own identity. The author's own experience in the American South leads him to believe that such possibilities exist among races in the United States. His research and experience motivate him to suggest that the same possibility may exist among the Slavs of the European South. Although we might like to know the answer to this difficult question after twenty-five years of socialist experience, we realize that many more decades may be involved. At the same time, we must not forget that while this study has shown that the system of values engendered by more education, exposure, and travel raises such possibilities, a reversal in the pattern must not be overlooked. Over the long run, any number of breaks and discontinuities can be expected. The nationalist escalation of the early 1970's is a good case in point. While the general mass trend may suggest one pattern, reversals can occur since the future is not likely to follow one continual, linear process.

It is clear that the system of values conducive to community development could not be brought about with the individual skills and facilities for social communication found in pre-war Yugoslavia. The evolution of such values requires the presence of a population that has the ability to communicate and an environment with the structures and institutions that encourage interchange and cooperation in all areas of social, political, and economic affairs. The post-war Communist system has encouraged the evolution of such a population and has provided an environment that has engendered the evolution of such values. It remains to be seen how much time these values will be given to evolve, and further, what strength and intensity of values will be needed to counter the potentially disintegrative tendencies that the system might incur. The answers to these questions will provide some important insights into the future of the Yugoslav experiment.

APPENDIX A

Guttman Scale of Modernism-Traditionalism

The scale was formed from five evaluative statements with four-point, agree-disagree response categories. The five items, marginals, and coefficient of reproducibility for the country-wide sample are as follows:

English Translation of Evaluative Statements from Original Survey Instrument	Percent of Overall Sample Responding in Agreement Categories
1) If you don't keep all four eyes open, people will exploit and deceive you.	74
2) The most important thing for children is that they learn to obey their parents.	66
3) In order to fulfill their personal goals and personal desires, individuals must compete and subdue one another.	49
4) The world is governed by supernatural forces which predetermine the course of events.	23
5) The children of great people are endowed with the qualities of their parents.	17

Coefficient of Reproducibility = 92.5

APPENDIX B

Guttman Scale of Cultural Universalism-Particularism

The scale was formed from five evaluative statements with four-point, agree-disagree response categories. The five items, marginals, and coefficient of reproducibility for the country-wide sample are as follows:

English Translation of Evaluative Statements from Original Survey Instrument	Percent of Overall Sample Responding in Agreement Categories
1) It is important to know the history of your family.	89
2) It is important for a man to speak his own dialect.	68
3) Nationality is important in our country.	54
4) It is better that a judge whom you know pass judgment on you, for example from your own locale, than to be judged by someone you do not know.	33
5) It is not necessary to talk with individuals whose thoughts are in opposition to ours.	21

Coefficient of Reproducibility = 91.7

APPENDIX C

Scale of Ethnic Distance

The six questions asked the 2600 respondents were:

1. Are you (e.g., a Slovene respondent), in favor of his (e.g., a Macedonian) permanent residence in your republic?
2. Are you in favor of his employment in the organization where you are employed?
3. Would you accept him as a friend?
4. Would you agree to marry him or her?
5. Would you accept him as your manager at the place where you work?
6. Would you be in favor of his holding a leading office in your republic?

The six questions were asked in respect to the following eight groups (excluding the respondent's own group): Serbs, Croats, Slovenes, Macedonians, Montenegrins, Albanians, Hungarians, Moslems.

NOTES

CHAPTER I

1. In the foreword to the special issue on "Political Integration in Multi-National States," the editor writes: "If anyone should doubt that political integration in multinational states is far from being a given attribute on the world stage today, he need only reflect on some of the events of recent years." *Journal of International Affairs*, XXVII, 1 (1973), p. xi.

2. Following the conception of Karl Deutsch, community may be defined as a grouping of people who have learned to communicate and cooperate with each other and to understand each other beyond the normal interchange of goods and services. Karl Deutsch, *Nationalism and Social Communication* (Cambridge, Mass.: MIT Press, 1966), p. 78. Community-building is used in this essay to refer to any developments conducive to such communication, cooperation, and understanding. For a similar conception, see: Kenneth Jowitt. *Revolutionary Breakthroughs and National Development* (Berkeley: University of California Press, 1971), p. 74. Jowitt writes: "Community-building will refer to attempts at creating new political meanings which are shared by elites and publics and which possess an informal, expressive, and institutional character."

3. For a fine historical and constitutional analysis of the Yugoslav idea. see: Frits W. Hondius, *The Yugoslav Community of Nations* (The Hague: Mouton, 1968).

4. For an overview of the national problem and resultant difficulties, see: Stephen Clissold (ed.), *A Short History of Yugoslavia* (Cambridge: Cambridge University Press, 1966), pp. 154-208.

5. For an excellent analysis of the nationalities policies of the Titoist regime, including the various changes over the years, see: Paul Shoup, *Communism and the Yugoslav National Question* (New York: Columbia University Press, 1968).

6 See discussions of the amendments in : Paul Shoup, "The National Question in Yugoslavia," *Problems of Communism*, XXI (Jan.-Feb., 1972), pp. 25-27; and R. V. Burks, *The National Problem and the Future of Yugoslavia*, The Rand Corporation, October, 1971 pp. 31-39.

7. *Borba*, June 28, 1972.

8. In his article on the nationalities question in the Yugoslav journal *Gledišta*, Yugoslav scholar and party ideologist, Stipe Šuvar, writes in his opening sentence: "There is no doubt that in Yugoslavia in 1971, the main theme in political life is the nationalities question." Stipe Šuvar, "Marginal Notes on the Nationalities Question," *Gledišta*, No. 5-6 (1971), p. 47. This and three other articles by Yugoslav scholars appearing in this issue of *Gledišta* have been translated and are reprinted in the special issue "The Nationalities Question in Yugoslavia," *International Journal of Politics*, II (Spring, 1972).

CHAPTER II

1. Belief system is defined as a configuration of values and attitudes which defines an individual's approach to human experience. The entire configuration will be beyond the scope of this analysis; however, a considerable number of attitudes closely related to the community-building process will be considered in the study.

2. Gabriel A. Almond and Sidney Verba, *The Civic Culture* (Boston: Little Brown and Company, Inc., 1965), p. 43.

3. For reports of each of the efforts, see respectively: Daniel Lerner, *The Passing of Traditional Society* (Glencoe, Ill.: The Free Press, 1958); for a brief report of the Center for International Affairs's project and an article based on its findings, see Alex Inkeles, "Making Men Modern: On the Causes and Consequences of Individual Change in Six Developing Countries," *American Journal of Sociology*, LXXV (September, 1969), pp. 208-225; and Almond, *Civic Culture*.

4. The term social is used to describe phenomena pertaining to large sectors of Yugoslav society. For example, the phenomena of relevance to this study, i.e., increasing levels of education, exposure to the mass media, and travel rates, are considered to be elements of social change because they are affecting a considerable portion of the Yugoslav populace.

5. Forecasts by Yugoslav economists note that these changes (e.g., education increases) will continue for an indefinite period of time along with further economic development.

6. Since statistical projections ascertain that these social changes will be reaching increasingly larger numbers of the Yugoslav populace as time passes, any effect associated with these changes can be projected to the future.

7. For a distinction between "micropolitics" and "macropolitics," see: Almond, *Civic Culture*, pp. 30-35.

8. Shoup, *Communism and the Yugoslav National Question*, p. 262.

9. For a conception distinguishing between *narod* and *nacije*, see: Ante Fiamengo, *Osnovi Opće Sociologije* ("Foundations of General Sociology") (Sarajevo: Veselin Masleša, 1963), pp. 219-231. Professor Fiamengo views *narod* as a transitional state between tribe and nation. Whereas a *narod* is not bound by links of blood relationship as tribes are, it does not enjoy the same level of autonomy and self-sufficiency as a nation. Therefore, *nacije* is often viewed as a more developed and autonomous state of a *narod*.

10. For some uses of the term nation-building in other settings, see Karl W. Deutsch and William J. Foltz, *Nation-Building* (New York: Atherton Press, 1963); Lucien W. Pye, *Politics, Personality and Nation-Building: Burma's Search for Identity* (New Haven: Yale University Press, 1962); Arnold Rivkin, "The Politics of Nation-Building: Problems and Preconditions," *Journal of International Affairs*, XVI, No. 2 (1962), pp. 131-143; and Stein Rokkan, "Models and Methods in the Comparative Study of Nation-Building," *Acta Sociologica*, XII, No. 2 (1969), pp. 53-73.

11. J. V. Stalin, *Marxism and the National Question* (New York: International Publishers, 1942), p. 16.

12. The exact number of nations in modern Yugoslavia is somewhat unclear and depends of course upon the criteria used for defining nations. Five people have traditionally been ascribed national status—Slovene, Croat, Serb, Montenegrin, and Macedonian—and the idea has lately been gaining acceptance with two others— *Muslimani* (or Bosnian) and Albanian.

13. See, for example, Hondius' choice of terms in *The Yugoslav Community of Nations*.

14. Edvard Kardelj, *Ravoj Slovenačkog Nacionalnog Pitanja* ("Development of the Slovene Nation Question") (2nd ed.; Belgrade: Kultura, 1958), p. 104.

15. Paul Shoup argues that Kardelj's work was not a defense of the right and integrity of Yugoslav nations (republics)—as he contends it is mistakenly interpreted by many Yugoslavs—but rather a basis for resisting the "internationalism" emanating from Moscow. For a detailed explanation of the idea, see: Shoup, *Communism and the Yugoslav National Question*, pp. 203-207.

16. See, for example, the implications raised by Kardelj as regards the Yugoslav nations on the following pages: Kardelj, *Razoj Slovenačkog Nacionalnog Pitanja*, pp. 39, 53.

17. The following works offer exhaustive analysis of the terms nation, nationalism, and other closely associated words. Hans Kohn, *Nationalism: Its Meaning and History* (Princeton: D. Van Nostrand, Co., Inc., 1955); Boyd C. Shafer, *Nationalism: Myth and Reality* (New York: Harcourt, Brace and Co., 1955); Louis Snyder, *The Meaning of Nationalism* (New Brunswick, N. J.: Rutgers University Press, 1954); and Louis L. Snyder, ed., *The Dynamics of Nationalism* (New York, D. Van Nostrand Co., Inc., 1964); and Deutsch, *Nationalism and Social Communication*.

18. The question in Yugoslavia of whether or not a grouping of people deserve the title of *narod, nacije, ethnička grupa,* or some lesser notation is still not entirely clear. Esad Ćimić notes, for example, that the *Muslimani* in Bosnia-Hercegovina have been called any number of lesser terms ranging from *"ethnička zajednica"* ("ethnic community") to *"muslimanska narod"* ("Moslem peoples"). However, he notes that with the publication of *Nacionalni i Politički Razvitak Muslimana* and *Muslimani Srpskohrvatskog Jezika,* the association of the word "nation" with the *Muslimani* no longer represents a "taboo idea" in Yugoslavia. See Ćimić's review of the former book in *Naše Teme,* II (February, 1970), pp. 420-424. For the two books using the term "nation" to describe the Muslimani, see: Atif Purivatra, *Nacionalni i Politički Razvitak Muslimana* ("National and Political Development of the Moslem Slavs") (Sarajevo: Svjetlost, 1969); and Salema Ćerića, *Muslimani Srpskohrvatskog Jezika* ("Moslem Serbo-Croatian Language") (Sarajevo: Svjetlost, 1969).

19. The idea of nation-building does not imply that the nation is inevitably involved in a process of further development. In fact, it may well be that the nations of Yugoslavia are undergoing a process of deterioration at the expense of the larger socialist community. In other words, such terms as nation- and community-building can denote growth, equilibrium, or decline.

20. Although it has been extremely uncommon in the past, the two recent analyses cited earlier refer to the *Muslimani* sector of Bosnia-Hercegovina in terms of national status. See: Purivatra, *Nacionalni Razvitak Muslimana;* and Ćerića, *Muslimani Jezika.*

21. Ćimić offers the following three alternative solutions to resolve the national question in Bosnia-Hercegovina: 1) United Bosnia nation—Ćimić's research indicates that this solution is accepted by the *Muslimani* but rejected by the Serb and Croat elements; 2) Three separate nations of Serbs, Croats, and *Muslimani*—this solution would have a disintegrative effect on the republic; 3) Three separate peoples—this solution, incidentally, which Ćimić favors—recognizes national differences but remains flexible enough for possible national integration in the future. Esad Ćimić, "Nacija u Svjetlu Sociološke Analize" ("Nation in the Light of Sociological Analysis"), *Sociologija,* XI, No. 3 (1969), pp. 402-403.

22. For an account of the development of this nationality within Yugoslavia, see: Predrag Ajtic, "Osobnosti Društvenog Razvitka Albanske Narodnosti u SFRJ: Aktuelni Problemi Njenog Daljeg Razvitka" ("The Individual Social Development of the Albanian nationality in Yugoslavia: Current Problems of its Further Development"), *Političke Sveske,* I (1969), pp. 101-114.

23. Although a considerable number of citizens, particularly the younger sectors, seem to be identifying themselves as Yugoslavs, it is still an "undesirable" category because it "renounces" one's national heritage. However, with increasing intermarriage, and the resultant problem of choosing between the nationality of mother and father, the size of the "Yugoslav" category is likely to grow.

24. Graham Wallace, *Human Nature in Politics* (New York: Alfred A. Knopf. Inc., 1921), pp. 286-287.

25. For an extremely interesting analysis of this assimilation or "homogenesis" process in Yugoslavia by one of their leading social scientists, see: Ruža Petrovic, "Ethno-Biološko Homogenizacija Jugoslovenskog Društva" ("The Ethnological-Biological Homogenesis of Yugoslav Society"), *Sociologija,* X, No. 2 (1968), pp. 5-35. Professor Petrović uses official Yugoslav statistics on the nationality of marriage partners to suggest that there is indeed a process of "ethnological mixing" going on in Yugoslavia today. She finds the rate of the "homogenesis" process to be dependent upon three different forms of "closeness": 1) territorial nearness, 2) similarity or closeness of social characteristics, and 3) similarity of cultural traits. As each of these forms of differentiation are diminished by increased commjunication and travel, the Yugoslavs' effort to abolish social differentiation, and the unavoidable twentieth century cultural movement toward a new "mass culture," the rate of this process *may* be likely to increase.

26. Deutsch, *Nationalism and Social Communication,* p. 105.

27. Edvard Kardelj, *O Osnovama Društvenog i Političkog Uredjenja FNRJ* ("Social and Political Arrangements of Yugoslavia")(Belgrade: Kultura, 1953), pp. 51-52.

28. See, for example, Shoup's account that notes the national fragmentation during the interwar years. Shoup, *Communism and the Yugoslav National Question*, pp. 13-59.

29. For separate and in-depth consideration of each of these factors, as well as their relationahips to Yugoslav development, see: M. George Zaninovich, *The Development of Socialist Yugoslavia* (Baltimore: The Johns Hopkins Press, 1968). Zaninovich identifies separate periods of post-war Yugoslav development and considers a number of ideological and environmental determinants and concomitants of each phase.

30. Otto Bauer, *Die Nationalitätenfrage und die Sozialdemokratie* ("The Nationality Question and Social Democracy") (2nd ed.; Vienna: Verlag der Wiener Volksbuchhandlung, 1924), p. 135.

31. Don Luigi Sturzo, *Nationalism and Internationalism* (New York: Roy Publishers, 1946) pp. 16-17.

32. Shoup, *Communism and the Yugoslav National Question*, p. 186.

33. Deutsch, *Nationalism and Social Communication*, p. 89.

34. The definitions are numerous and seldom similar. After considering ninety-four definitions of community, G. A. Hillery concluded that, "beyond the concept that people are involved in community, there is no complete agreement as to the nature of community." George A. Hillery, "Definitions of Community: Areas of Agreement," *Rural Sociology*, XX (June, 1955), p. 119.

35. Quincy Wright, *A Study of War*, abrid. by Louise Leonard Wright (Chicago: The University of Chicago Press, 1964), p. 240.

36. *Ibid.*, p. 214-215.

37. *Ibid.*, p. 215.

38. Deutsch, *Nationalism and Social Communication*, p. 91.

39. Rupert Emerson, *From Empire to Nation* (Cambridge, Mass.: Harvard University Press, 1960), p. 95.

40. For purposes of this study, however, one more characteristic is added to his definition. Namely, when nation is used to refer to the broader Yugoslav population in this study, it will mean a community of people with a common heritage and common destiny bound by a common set of political structures.

41. It should be clear by this point that the study will be considering simultaneously a number of different change processes. The initial process, social and economic development, is viewed as affecting the individual. This resultant process, referred to as "individual change," is viewed as a determinant of the more restricted community-building process. Because of their close relationship in Yugoslav development, it is mandatory to consider all of them. However, social and economic develop-

ment will receive minor attention and will be mentioned only in regard to their effect on the process of individual change.

42. F. E. Ian Hamilton, *Yugoslavia: Patterns of Economic Activity* (London: G. Bell and Sons, Ltd., 1968), pp. 116-117.

43. Official Yugoslav statistics clearly show the trends in each of these general areas of change. For a sound empirical treatment of this change in social structure and mobility, but as it relates more directly to the working class, see: Miloš Ilić, ed., *Socijalna Struktura i Pokretljivost Radničke Klase Jugoslavije* ("Social Structure and Mobility of the Working Class of Yugoslavia") (Beograd: Institut Društvenih Nauka, 1963).

44. The work force employed in agricultural occupations has dropped from as high as eighty per cent before the war to a figure now approaching forty per cent.

45. One of Lerner's basic propositions is that "*mobility tends to be systemic*, i.e., physical, social and psychic mobility 'go together.' " Lerner, *Passing of Traditional Society*, p. 132.

46. *Ibid*.

47. For a useful review of the literature on industrialization and urbanization, especially as related to their effects on changing family structure, behavior, and value systems, see: Joseph A. Kahl, "Some Social Concomitants of Industrialization and Urbanization," *Human Organization*, XVIII (Summer, 1959), pp. 53-74.

48. The Statistical Yearbook has shown general increases in each of these indicators after the post-war years. See the figures in *Statistički Godišnjak*, published annually from 1954 to the present.

49. Philip Converse finds that the degree of interrelatedness within belief systems, or as Converse calls it, "the degree of contraint among idea-elements," is higher among elite than cross-section samples in the United States. The same probably applies to Yugoslav samples. Philip E. Converse, "The Nature of Belief Systems in Mass Publics," in David E. Apter, ed., *Ideology and Discontent* (London: The Free Press of Glencoe, 1964), pp. 227-234.

50. As will be explained in detail later, this study of individual characteristics is based upon survey data gathered by the Center for Public Opinion Research in Belgrade.

51. The Harvard Project on the Social and Cultural Aspects of Economic Development found that this perspective or "structure" of the traditional to modern phenomena is basically the same in all of the six diverse countries they studied. Inkeles notes: "The psychological 'structure' of individual modernity is basically very much the same in all six of the very different countries we studied." Alex Inkeles, "Participant Citizenship in Six Developing Countries," *American Political Science Review*, LXIII (December, 1969), p. 1121.

52. The universalism-particularism formulation of Parsons and Shils is of course relevant here. See, for example, their conceptualizations of the differences between

the orientations of the universalistic and particularistic actors: Talcott Parsons and Edward A. Shils, *Toward a General Theory of Action* (Cambridge, Mass.: Harvard University Press, 1951).

53. The theoretical and empirical basis for using these two variables and also the social mobilization variable will be discussed in detail in a later chapter.

54. Karl W. Deutsch, "Social Mobilization and Political Development," *American Political Science Review*, IV (September, 1961), p. 493.

55. Deutsch, *Nation-Building*, p. 6.

56. *Ibid.*, pp. 7-8.

57. Lerner, *Passing of Traditional Society*.

58. *Ibid.*, p. 60.

59. *Ibid.*, p. 69.

60. *Ibid.*, p. 52.

61. Almond and Verba, *Civic Culture*.

62. Norman H. Nie, G. Bingham Powell, Jr., and Kenneth Prewitt, "Social Structure and Political Participation, I and II," *American Political Science Review*, LXII, LXIII (June and September, 1969), pp. 361-379 and 808-832, respectively.

63. *Ibid.*, p. 808.

64. See: Deutsch, *Nationalism and Social Communication*, esp. pp. 86-101.

65. *Ibid.*, p. 87.

66. For some of Deutsch's applications, see: "The Growth of Nations: Some Recurrent Patterns of Political and Social Intregration," *World Politics*, V (January, 1953), pp. 168-195; and "Social Mobilization and Political Development," pp. 493-514.

67. Although rather limited use of survey research has been made among researchers specifically interested in community-building, there are some notable exceptions in the general area of modernization and socio-economic development. See, for example: Michael Armer and Al Nauman, "Individual Modernization and Psychological Alienation," (unpublished paper prepared for the American Sociological Association Meeting, 1967); L. W. Doob, *Becoming More Civilized: A Psychological Explanation* (New Haven, Yale University Press, 1960), and Doob, *Patriotism and Nationalism: Their Psychological Foundations* (New Haven: Yale University Press, 1964).

68. The ecological fallacy results when trying to make inferences about individuals when using social or aggregate level data. For a discussion, see: W. S. Robinson, "Ecological Correlations and the Behavior of Individuals," *American Sociological Review*, XV (1950), pp. 351-357.

69. For articles based upon the research, see: Inkeles, "Making Men Modern," pp. 208-225, and "Participant Citizenship in Six Developing Countries," pp. 1120-1142.

70. Inkeles, "Making Men Modern," p. 213.

71. *Ibid.*, p. 213.

72. The reader is reminded of Lerner's account of the "Grocer" and the "Chief" and his use of their characteristics to convey the change taking place in the Middle East. Also, Schramm tells about two families, the Ifes and the Bvanis, to convey the "human meaning of under-development." In this section, the author will relate his friendship with two individuals to convey some of the human problems and possibilities of individual change and community-building in Yugoslavia. For the accounts of Lerner and Schramm, see: Lerner, *Passing of Traditional Society*, pp. 19-42; and Wilbur Schramm, *Mass Media and National Development* (Stanford, Calif.: Stanford University Press, 1964), pp. 1-19.

73. The survey data mentioned are those collected by the Center for Public Opinion Research in Belgrade. The data were collected under the sponsorship of Professor M. George Zaninovich and served as the data base for his research project entitled "Value Change in Yugoslav Society." The author gratefully acknowledges the financial support of the Project on the Comparative Study of Communist Societies, University of California, Berkeley, California in carrying out this project, and also his appreciation to Professor Zaninovich for use of the survey data. It should be noted at this juncture that these data will serve as a basis for the empirical analysis to follow in later chapters. For a consideration of the sample, sampling techniques, and other questions related to the data, the reader is asked to refer to Chapter III.

74. This source was not used to lend support to the findings of the study or to prove or disprove any hypotheses. The value of the source is in its ability to prevent the researcher from becoming too detached or removed from reality. Too often survey data are collected, analyzed, and reported with little sensitivity to or deeper appreciation of the individuals from whom the data was collected. This short narrative is only intended to show that the data have "relevance" to the author's concern with community-building in the Yugoslav context.

75. For the evidence of this universal phenomenon, see: Alfred Metraux, *Race and Civilization* (Paris: UNESCO, 1950).

CHAPTER III

1. The interviewing and study, directed by Professor M. George Zaninovich and part of his larger study entitled "Value Change in Yugoslav Society," was carried out through the services of the Centar za Istraživanje Javnog Mnenja (Center for Research of Public Opinion) in Belgrade. The Center, directed and staffed by well-trained survey researchers, regularly carries on research of its own bearing, for other Yugoslav scientists, and for numerous foreign organizations and individuals.

2. As was noted in the preceding chapters, the percentage of television viewers, radio listeners, and newspaper readers is increasing yearly in the country. For some interesting ideas about the possible effect of this phenomenon, see: Ivan Kuvačić, "Masovne Komunikacije i Suvremeno Društvo" ("Mass Communications and Contemporary Society"), *Sociologija*, X, No. 4 (1968), pp. 5-19.

3. This relationship is the central thesis of Deutch's book. He writes: "The community which permits a common history to be experienced as common, is a community of complementary habits and facilities of communication. It requires, so to speak, equipment for the job. This job consists in the storage, recall, transmission, recombination, and reapplication of relatively wide ranges of information." See: Deutsch, *Nationalism and Social Communication*, p. 96.

4. Lerner's "traditional" man was not only unable to view the world in this manner, but was afraid to try. Lerner, *Passing of Traditional Society*, pp. 45-52. A man without this capacity is an individual with a relatively low level of information intake. Current questions in one's social life are perceived and acted upon on the basis of stored information. If this level is low, and further, if it consists of only information gained from limited sources, one's capacity for understanding complex human relations is low. This suggests the dynamic of the learning process. As social and economic change continues, individuals inevitably come in contact with more and increasingly diverse kinds of information.

5. It should be noted that this conception of mobilization is substantially different from the phenomena surrounding the discussion of "mobilization systems" or the discussion concerning the use of mass organizations (e.g., the Communist party) as "mobilizing agents." Whereas the phenomenon we are interested in focuses upon the individual level of analysis, the mobilization systems of Apter and others focus on the social level. Apter illustrates his interest in the societal unit when he writes that mobilization systems "emphasize the rebirth and regeneration of the *community through the combined action of the whole*," (Italics mine) in David Apter, *The Politics of Modernization* (Chicago: The University of Chicago Press, 1965), p. 360.

6. Deutsch, *Nationalism and Social Communication*, p. 126.

7. For convenience in presentation, the continuum-type modernism-particularism scale will be referred to as *modernism*. The next scale to be discussed, cultural universalism-particularism, will be shortened to *universalism*.

8. Lerner, *Passing of Traditional Society*, pp. 45-49.

9. See Appendix A for a complete listing of the items, marginals, and coefficient of reproducibility. For a discussion of the four scaling criteria and the procedures for Guttman scaling in general, see: Robert N. Ford, "A Rapid Scoring Procedure for Scaling Attitude Questions," *Public Opinion Quarterly*, XIV (Fall, 1950), pp. 507-532. Also, it should be noted that Guttman scales constructed from five items yield thirty-one unique scores. However, in the two scales used in this study the collapsing technique suggested by Ford was employed to give six-category scales.

10. The five attitudes used to construct this Guttman scale were originally identified through a factor analysis of thirty-eight value statements in the questionnaire. These five items, along with five items comprising the Cultural Universalism Particularism scale to be discussed in the next paragraph, originally clustered into one factor. However, upon examining the factor we identified two logically and, as later analysis indicated, empirically separate components. That is, five items clearly reflected a "modern-traditional syndrome," while another five pointed to elements of universalism and particularism within the Yugoslav setting. The author decided to submit both of the two separate components to Guttman analysis and found that both easily surpassed the criteria prescribed for scalability. Also, it should be noted that the factor containing these ten items was the most "powerful" of all delineated factors. That is, it explained more variation in the total grouping of thirty-eight attitudes than any other factor. Therefore, in addition to the clear intuitive significance of the ten value statements, factor analysis has pointed to their empirical importance in "explaining" the belief systems of the 1186 respondents. For an article that suggests submitting survey data to both Guttman and factor analysis, see Jeanne E. Gullahorn and John T. Gullahorn, "The Utility of Applying Both Guttman and Factor Analysis to Survey Data," *Sociometry*, XXXI (June, 1968), pp. 213-219.

11. Each of the analyses points to the potential sources of particularism present within different social settings and discusses the implications that such particularism raises. See: Charles W. Anderson, Fred R. von der Mehden, and Crawford Young, *Issues of Political Development* (Englewood Cliffs, N. J.: Prentice-Hall, Inc., 1967), pp. 20-60; Edward Shils, "Primordial, Personal, Sacred and Civil Ties," *British Journal of Sociology* (June, 1957); and Clifford Geertz, "The Integrative Revolution: Primordial Sentiments and Civil Politics in the New States," in Geertz, ed., *Old Societies and New States* (New York: The Free Press of Glencoe, Inc., 1963), pp. 111-117.

12. Deutsch remarks, "Peoples are marked off from each other by communication barriers, by 'marked gaps' in the efficiency of communication." Deutsch, *Nationalism and Social Communication.*, p. 100.

13. See Appendix B for a listing of the items forming the scale, the marginals, and the coefficient of reproducibility.

14. The question of language remains an unsolved question even in present-day Yugoslavia. The 1954 Novi Sad agreement on the "merger" to form the Serbo-Croatian language has been under continued criticism from certain segments of the society. Exemplary was the incident in Spring, 1967, when most important cultural organizations in Croatia signed a resolution repudiating the Novi Sad agreement and, in effect, argued for a stricter separation of the two languages. For an analysis of the language issue, see: Thomas Magner, "Language and Nationalism in Yugoslavia" *Canadian Slavic Studies*, I (Fall, 1967), pp. 333-347.

15. For a discussion of the importance of the family unit in Yugoslavia, see: Vera St. Erlich, *Family in Transition* (Princeton: Princeton University Press, 1966), pp. 21-59, *passim*, and, Jozo Tomasevich, *Peasants, Politic, and Economic Change in Yugoslavia* (Stanford: Stanford University Press, 1955), pp. 178-189.

16. See, for example, the chapter "The Reshaping of the Family," in Erlich, *Family in Transition*, pp. 413-451.

17. Anderson, *et. al.*, use the term "sub-national" loyalties to refer to this set of particularlistic phenomena. "Through a close examination of the emergence of sub-national loyalties, we may begin to establish some baselines for fixing at least the general direction of change." Anderson, *Issues of Political Development*, p. 28.

18. The Guttman approach necessitates asking questions about the same theme. For example, for this study such questions as the following were asked to give a general measure of universalism-particularism in Yugoslavia: Do you think you could get a fair trial outside of your own locale? Is nationality important in your country? Is it important for a man to speak his own dialect? Is it necessary to speak with individuals whose thoughts (value systems) are in opposition to yours? Is it important to know the history of your family?

19. It is necessary to note that the phrasing of statements such as those representing the two Guttman scales will of course affect the importance a respondent attaches to them. However, for the purposes of Guttman scaling, the phrasing of the question is not important as long as the statement yields the required range in marginals. What is important is the fact that each question was phrased in the same manner for all 1186 respondents. For the requirements of a Guttman scale and the four criteria for scalability, refer to: Ford, "Scaling Attitude Questions," pp. 507-527.

20. Lerner, *Passing of Traditional Society*, pp. 43-55; Inkeles, "Making Men Modern," pp. 208-225.

21. The reader is reminded of Lerner's central proposition, i.e., "physical, social and psychic mobility 'go together'." Lerner, *Passing of Traditional Society*, p. 132.

22. For empirical support of this relationship, see the literature summarized in the section, "Determinants of Intergroup Attitudes," in John Harding, *et. al.*, "Prejudice and Ethnic Relations," in Gardner Lindzey, ed., *Handbook of Social Psychology* (2 vol.; Reading, Mass.: Addison-Wesley Publishing Co., 1954), I, pp. 1038-1046.

23. This conception of change would fall into the "evolutionist" category. For a discussion of this category and other classifications of change theorists, see: Max Heirich, "Use of Time in the Study of Social Change," *American Sociological Review*, XXIX (June, 1964), pp. 386-397. For a discussion of the "evolutionists," see pp. 391-393.

24. It is simply impossible to conceive of a Slovene and a Macedonian feeling part of the same community when some isolated sectors have had no knowledge of the identification or where-abouts of the other group. This condition was not uncommon in the past. Today, however, "Television Skopje" broadcasts daily to Ljubljana, and "Television Ljubljana" to Skopje. In other words, as the country increasingly assumes the features of a technological, "cybernetic" society, the citizenry has the opportunity to learn more about other sectors in the country.

25. As evaluated in terms of the survey questionnaire, the traditionalistic and particularistic man in the study contends that "if you don't keep all four eyes open in our society, people will exploit and deceive you," and that, "it is not necessary to speak with individuals whose thoughts are in opposition to ours." These of course are not the type of values conducive to the development of a larger cooperative, socialist community.

26. This has not always been the case in this part of the Balkans. For an extreme but enlightening comparison of "political styles," note the differences in the tone and style of recent parliamentary or assembly meetings as compared with those between the two World Wars. We will remember the "Škupština Murders" ("Assembly Murders") of 1928 when a Montenegrin deputy (Račić) pulled his revolver in the Assembly and killed two Croatian deputies and mortally wounded the Croat Peasant Party leader, Stjepan Radić. For an account of this period, see: Clissold, *Short History of Yugoslavia*, pp. 170-208. Today, the Assembly delegates generally couch their needs and demands in a rather different fashion. In short, the "political arena" may be taking on a more conciliatory atmosphere.

27. This idea has definite application in many countries, from those commonly referred to as more developed to those thought of as less developed. Evidence of racial unrest in the United States, religious in Ireland, and tribal in Nigeria suggest that these countries are perhaps communicating but certainly not fully cooperating and understanding. Accordingly, although levels of mobilization and modernization are high (at least in the first two), there is perhaps a "lag" in terms of particularistic orientations. Namely, race in the United States, religion in Ireland, and tribe in Nigeria are loyalties suggesting particularistic attitudes that are impeding understanding and cooperation and hence the development of "community." The model here, however, is designed more narrowly for Yugoslavia, and attempts to reflect the unique background and contemporary environment surrounding its development.

28. See Herman Wold and Lars Jureen, *Demand Analysis* (New York: John Wiley and Sons, 1953), pp. 48-57 for a discussion of "structural systems."

29. For a full explanation of "recursive systems," see: Hubert Blalock, *Causal Inferences in Non-Experimental Research* (Chapel Hill: The University of North Carolina Press, 1961)., pp. 52-60. Since the word "cause" is used occasionally in the formulations, it should be noted that the term is used with the discretion outlined by Blalock. He writes: "it is quite correct that one can never demonstrate causality from correlational data, or in fact from any type of empirical information. Nevertheless, it is possible to make causal inferences concerning the adequacy of causal models, at least in the sense that we can proceed by eliminating inadequate models that make predictions that are not consistent with the data. As we have seen, such causal models involve (1) a definite set of explicitly defined variables, (2) certain assumptions about how these variables are interrelated causally, and (3) assumptions to the effect that outside variables, while operating, do not have confounding influences that disturb the causal patterning among the variable explicitly being considered. *Ibid.*, p. 62.

30. e_1 refers to the effects of all outside variables (e.g., economic development) on a particular variable (in this case, social mobilization). b refers to the regression coefficient (slope), or in other words, the rate of change in one variable per unit of change in another.

31. In other words, this study is not concerned empirically with the particular causes of A (which we earlier acknowledged to be increased social and economic development) but rather with the effects of A, i.e., B and C.

32. It is of course logically possible that b_{21} is zero, that A_1 does not bring about B_2, and that both A_1 and B_2 are exogenous variables caused by factors outside the system. However, the data analysis to follow will disconfirm this possibility.

33. See: Frederick Harbison and Charles A. Myers, *Education, Man-power, and Economic Growth: Strategies of Human Resource Development* (New York: McGraw Hill, 1964), p. 181.

CHAPTER IV

1. The reader is reminded that Lerner's conception of modernization referred to the "infusion of a rationalist and positivist spirit." Lerner, *Passing of Traditional Society*, p. 45. It may be argued that this definition conveys a certain degree of Western bias. However, the applicability of the concept in the Yugoslav context is based upon two different sets of rationale. The first represents the findings of the cross-national studies of Lerner and Inkeles. Lerner contends that, "the same basic model reappears in virtually all modernizing societies on all continents of the world regardless of variations in race, color, creed." *Ibid.*, p. 46. Inkeles similarly notes that "the psychological 'structure' of individual modernity is basically very much the same in all six of the very different countries we studied." Inkeles, "Participant Citizenship," p. 1121. The second reason for using this definition is based upon the findings of various Yugoslav scientists concerned with the process of cultural and individual change. See, for example: Erlich, *Family in Transition*; and Dunja Rightman-Augustin, "Tradicionalna Kultura i Suvremene Vrednote" ("Traditional Culture and Contemporary Values") in Vladimir Milanović, *et. al.*, eds., *Kultura Razvoj Savremenog Jugoslovenskog Društva* ("Culture and Development of Contemporary Yugoslav Society"), (Split: Jugoslovensko Udruženje za Sociologiju, 1970), pp. 1-13. Therefore, values were selected that corresponded with the general formulations of Lerner and Inkeles and then were appraised on the basis of Yugoslav conceptualizations.

2. Guttman scaling and factor analyses of this system of values support the contention of Inkeles, when he states: "We . . . assume that this complex of attitudes and values holds together: that in the statistical sense it consitutes a factor, and a relatively coherent factor. In time, our scientific evidence will show whether or not this is a reasonable assumption." Inkeles,"Modernization of Man," p. 139. Statistical analysis of the set of values used in this study show that in the case of Yugoslavia this is in fact a reasonable assumption.

3. Inkeles talks about these forces in the following way: "So much for our conception of the qualities that make a man modern. What can we say about the forces that produce such a man, that most rapidly and effectively inculcate in a population those attitudes, values, needs, and ways of acting that better fit him for life in a modern society? Just as modernity seems to be defined not by any one characteristic, but by a complex of traits, so we find that no one social force, but rather a whole complex of influences, contributes to the transformation from traditional to modern man." *Ibid.*, p. 146. And then, he speaks of one of the "mobilizing" factors used in this study in the following manner. "Within this complex of forces, however, one certainly assumes pre-eminence: namely, education. Almost all serious scientific investigations of the question have shown the individual's degree of modernity to rise with increases in the amount of education he has received." *Ibid.*

4. For purposes of this question, Yugoslavia was divided into ten culture-regions which represented the six republics, the two autonomous regions (Vojvodina and Kosovo), Lika, and the Adriatic Coast.

5. This sector of Yugoslavia reminds the author of a story told by a former inhabitant of an isolated village whose population was characterized by very little travel and exposure. The elderly woman told of an African student who was passing through the village and decided to stop at a produce stand to purchase some fresh fruit. Upon climbing from the car, the black student was greeted by the shrieking of the attending peasant. "The devil has come, the devil has come!" Although this is a very atypical incident, it is worth noting that it is this kind of belief that results from not having traveled, not having read, viewed, or listened to the mass media, and not even having seen pictures that are commonly found in the "city magazines" circulating in the urban areas.

6. Nevesinje is located in the southern extreme of Bosnia-Hercegovina and is perhaps the least developed and most isolated commune represented in the study.

7. This trend is quickly changing, however, and increasing numbers are traveling to Hungary, Rumania, Bulgaria, and Greece, as well as to Western Europe. The lucrative exchange rate found for the Yugoslav dinar in the three Communist systems is becoming an increasingly inviting attraction for the Yugoslav tourist.

8. For an interesting analysis of Yugoslav mobility and travel patterns using the same survey data, see: C. R. Schuller, "Mobility and Social Values in Modern Yugoslavia," (unpublished paper, University of Oregon, 1969).

9. For Inkeles' contention, see: "Modernization of Man," p. 146.

10. It is interesting to note a similar reaction to an earthquake over 100 years ago, and incidentally, also among an Islamic community. In an article about traditionalism in two Islamic countries, Pfaff comments: "Rehabilitation efforts in Iran following the September 1862 earthquake were greatly impeded, for example, by the reluctance of the affected peasantry to accept responsibility for their own future and who preferred to resign their fate to Allah." Richard H. Pfaff, "Disengagement from Traditionalism in Turkey and Iran," *Western Political Quarterly*, XVI (March, 1963), p. 80. Later, he adds, "One of the most frequent expressions heard in the Middle East today is *inshallah*, or if God so wills." *Ibid.*

11. In regard to a strictly mechanical consideration, it should be noted that the manner of classifying the independent variables (i.e., the number of categories) in the three tables differs because of the various codifications found in the original survey instrument. In some cases, the original coded categories were collapsed for reasons of dispersion. Therefore, because the independent variables represent different phenomena, were coded in different ways, and revealed different patterns of dispersion, the low to high categories are classified differently in Tables 3, 4, and 5.

12. For broadcasting and television statistics for the country, see: *Statistički Kalendar Jugoslavije*, 1974, p. 117; also, for an investigation that represents an interesting attempt to establish the extent of dissemination by the different instruments of mass media in Yugoslavia, see: Firdus Džinić and Dragomir Pantić, "Rasiernost Politicko-Informativnog Dejstva Radija, Televizije i Štampe u SFRJ" ("The Dissemination of Political-Informative Influence by Radio, Television, and Newspapers in Yugoslavia"), *Izveštaji i Studije*, XVII (February, 1969). This study indicates that the instruments disseminate to a rather selective population within the country, and interestingly, that this receiving population coincides very closely with the "mobilized sector" of this study.

13. For an in-depth study of this relationship, see Erlich, *Family in Transition*, and especially the section entitled "The Status of the Father," pp. 60-94.

14. *Ibid.*, pp. 61-76. In one place she notes, "In an environment where life was changing rapidly, all 'inborn' authority vanished. The older folk strove to buttress the crumbling walls of the *zadruga* and patriarchal modes of life, trying so to speak to support them from the outside, but it rarely helped" (p. 75).

15. In another place Erlich talks about this form of traditionalism in the villages when quoting from the report of an interviewer in a district near Skopje: "The parents' authority is natural and not to be shaken . . . . The father's authority is maintained mainly by his superiority in experience and relations with others, while the children are cut off from everything and forced to be obedient." *Ibid.*, pp. 74-75.

16. According to an admittedly rough sample, the author finds a predominant portion of these "night owls" to be the sons and daughters of intellectuals, high government officials, and successful social and economic leaders within the community.

17. Lucien Pye notes that in most non-Western societies two distinct levels of communication exist—the urban level and the village level. The author's experiences in Yugoslavia show that these differences have considerable relevance in this environment. Pye writes: "In the urban center are the media of mass communication . . . . Outside these centers, the communication process is still largely dependent upon the traditional level of technology . . . . the pattern is usually further complicated by the fact that communication at the village level is largely dependent upon a word-of-mouth process." Lucien Pye, "Communication Patterns and the Problem of Representative Government in Non-Western Societies," *Public Opinion Quarterly*, 20 (Summer, 1956), pp. 250-251.

18. See, for example, Schramm's analysis of the drop in information flow as one moves from city to village in less developed countries. It perhaps should be acknowledged that this "drop-off" is not so great in Yugoslavia as in more under-developed societies, but it still represents a considerable contrast. Schramm remarks: "The significant point to note is how greatly the supply of information drops off between city and village in an underdeveloped country, and how relatively little it drops off in a highly developed country." Schramm, *Mass Media and National Development*, p. 70.

19. Alex Inkeles draws attention to the relationship between environment change and changing values in the following manner: "The characteristic mark of the modern man has two parts: one internal, the other external; one dealing with his environment, and the other with his attitudes, values, and feelings." Inkeles, "Modernization of Man," p. 139. As was argued earlier, it is unreasonable to expect man to "modernize" if the environment surrounding him is not. The fact that both environmental and human elements are *not* modernizing at the same high rate in the village as compared to more urban environments would seem clear at this point.

20. It is interesting, for example, to view the differences in this individual trait in Zagreb. With the influx of workers to the city, one finds the presence of a population speaking a number of dialects. Most members of the Croatian populace, however, are able to use the literary "štokavski" which is considerably easier for the foreign speaker

to understand since foreign instruction usually takes place in this dialect. However, the author found that some individuals would go to great lengths to avoid using the literary form, while others who also commonly used dialect forms would shift to it immediately upon finding that the author was not a native speaker.

21. It should be noted that when applying this control, the data indicate that most of the mobilized population tend to be both non-traditional and non-particularistic, while the non-mobilized group represents the opposite orientations. However, the data exhibit enough dispersion to show the relationships listed in Figure 6.

22. The author realizes that there may be deviations from this general trend. However, in statistical terms it is still a significant pattern. In later chapters, discussion will be directed toward different sectors of Yugoslav society which exhibit contrasting patterns within the general model. That is, by controlling for a number of variables such as nationality, level of socio-economic development, socio-political status, and so on, it will be possible to identify variations from the country-wide pattern by comparing correlation coefficients across the various control groups.

CHAPTER V

1. A Yugoslav ethnologist told the author that the two most important elements determining an individual's predisposition for value change within the modernizing Yugoslav environment are (1) his national heritage, and (2) the environmental setting in which he finds himself. Because of the general approval that this feeling receives on the part of other scholars familiar with the Yugoslav context, these two elements will be considered in this chapter. Other elements of relevance to the model, but perhaps of lesser importance, will be considered in the following chapter.

2. See Dzinić and Pantić, "Raširenost Dejstva," pp. 1-27, passim.

3. Erlich, Family in Transition, p. 376.

4. One must be careful where speaking about the "Oriental influenced" areas within the country. While the predominant portions of the southern and heartland sections were under Turkish domination and therefore influenced by "the Orient," some sections reacted very differently. That is, while some sectors became almost totally acculturated or "Islamized," others only lived and worked under the domain of the Sultan while rejecting his religion and much of his way of life. This fact has, of course, important implications for the phenomenon of individual value change.

5. The author's understanding of the area suggests that there is good reason for this idea, namely, when information levels are low and then increase rapidly, value change is extensive. However, if information levels are already high, another small increase in stimuli is unlikely to be of any major significance. Perhaps the following account provides an illustrative example. The author met peasant families who knew very little about Africa prior to one of Tito's visits to a number of African states. However, the families learned a great deal (and seemed to experience some change in attitudes) through the extensive television coverage provided on their recently acquired television sets. On the other hand, those with extensive prior information of Africa were probably unaffected, or at least to a lesser extent. The same influences can be observed in the broadcasts of domestic affairs, for example, the televising of Party congresses, of various cultural and informative programs, and so on.

6. George W. Hoffman and Fred Warner Neal, *Yugoslavia and the New Communism*, (New York: Twentieth Century Fund, 1962), p. 50.

7. Joel M. Halpern, *A Serbian Village*, (rev. ed.; New York: Harper and Row, 1967), pp. 291-292.

8. It would be interesting of course, to apply the model to all national groupings, e.g, Bosnians, Montenegrins, and so on, but because these samples become too small for purposes of statistical analysis, we will focus on the four largest populations. This does not seriously hamper the analysis, however, since these four populations represent almost the entire range in social, economic, and cultural characteristics found in the country.

9. These two communes represent less developed agricultural areas. Illustrative is the fact that eighty-four per cent of the inhabitants of Nevisinje and ninety-two per cent of those in Osečina were employed in the agricultural sector in 1971. Because of the relative isolation of the two communes and the lack of any industrial capabilities, the occupational structure of the communities remains relatively unchanged today.

10. In order to permit this sort of conceptual analysis, a ranking of the twenty-four communes was adopted that classified each unit according to an index of socio-economic development. This index takes into account an extensive number of social and economic indicators in the communes, combines them, and thereby allows the ranking of environments from the most highly developed to least developed. The author wishes to acknowledge that the index was constructed by Karl Johnson of the Department of Political Science, University of Missouri at Kansas City. For purposes of the control as used in this chapter, the ranking of the twenty-four communes has been "quartiled" to provide the following catefories: highly developed, developed, less developed, and least developed. This places six communes in each of the development categories.

11. It should be mentioned once again at this point that the sample design controlled for level of mobilization across nations and,therefore, produced national samples (i.e., Slovene, Croat, etc.) with relatively equal levels on the mobilization scale. Without this control, the ratio of mobilized to non-mobilized individuals would have been considerably higher among the nationalities from the more highly developed North (e.g., Slovenia and Croatia), and thereby, would have restricted cross-national analysis.

12. Perhaps it is necessary to inform the non-statistically oriented reader how to interpret the magnitude of the differences between the correlation coefficients of two different control groups. Since predicting an individual's rank on one ordinal scale (e.g., modernism) from knowledge of his rank on another (e.g., mobilization) is determined by the degree to which the two scales tend toward either agreement or inversion, the following interpretation is appropriate: since there is 40 per cent more agreement than inversion between the rankings of A and B among the country-wide sample (as reflected by the *gamma* coefficient of .40), and 31 per cent more agreement than inversion within the Slovene control group, it can be concluded that there are 9 more agreements per every 100 observations of the A-B relationship within the country-wide sample, than there are in the sample of Slovenes. In regard to another

methodological question, it is necessary to note that not enough is known about the sampling distribution of contingency measures to permit one to infer this same relative difference in coefficients to the larger populations. For a discussion of this issue, see: Hubert M. Blalock, Jr., *Social Statistics* (New York:McGraw-Hill Book Co., Inc., 1960), p. 311. This does not restrict the comparison of the relative size of two coefficients among the sample, but limits one's ability to infer that the same relative difference will exist among the broader populations. Blalock notes: "As long as he is content to describe relationships within his particular sample, he may simply compare the relative sizes of the two r's and note the magnitude of the difference. If he wishes to generalize to some larger population, however, the question will arise as to whether or not the obtained difference is likely to be due to chance." *Ibid.*, p. 309. This issue concerning the relative difference between the coefficients in two different samples should not, of course, be confused with tests of significance that establish the presence or absence of association between two variables within one sample.

13. This breakdown represents a simple dichotomization of the Guttman scale categories into two groups representing "traditional" and "modern."

14. Later sections, for example, will show that the same linkages within the Croat and Macedonian samples produce coefficients of .50 and .51, respectively.

15. This finding parallels the results of a study of "ethnic distance" in Yugoslavia. The study adapted the Bogardus "scale of social distance" to explore the attitudes of Yugoslavs toward other nationalities in the country. The results show that the Macedonians and Slovenes illustrate the highest level of rejection of other Yugoslav nationalities, while the Serbs and Croats display somewhat more tolerant values. For a report of this study in English see: Dragomir Pantić, "Ethnic Distance in Yugoslavia," *Yugoslav Fact and Values*, No. 53 (April, 1969), pp. 3-4.

16. In another study, the author has ranked all ethnic groups along a "Westernized" to "Easternized" dimension by analyzing an extensive number of attitudes. The ranking illustrated that the Slovenes are considerably more "Western" than any other Yugoslav population. See: Gary K. Bertsch, *Nation-Building in Yugoslavia: A Study of Political Integration and Attitudinal Consensus* (Beverly Hills: Sage Publications, 1971).

17. On the basis of projections using the 1971 census, the expectation is that there will be less than two million Slovenes in Yugoslavia in 1983. *Statistički Kalendar Jugoslavije*, 1974, p. 22.

18. It is interesting to note and fits with the findings that the data show the idea of nationality in Yugoslavia to be most strongly emphasized by the Slovenes and Macedonians. In response to the statement: "Nationality is important in our country," 54 per cent of the Slovenes and 52 per cent of the Macedonians strongly agreed, while only 30 per cent of the Serbs, and 32 per cent of the Croats responded in similar fashion.

19. When thought of in this fashion, the value systems can be closely tied to the idea of political culture. When using Verba's conception of political culture, i.e., "the system of beliefs, expressive symbols, and values which defines the setting in which political action takes place," the relevance becomes clear. See: Lucien Pye

and Sidney Verba, ed., *Political Culture and Political Development* (Princeton, New Jersey: Princeton Universtiy Press, 1965), p. 513.

20. It would be unrealistic to contend that the values defining the political setting in Yugoslavia will significantly lower the level of conflict within the system. However, the findings suggest that perhaps the values out of which political conflicts arise will tend to be based less upon the elements represented in the Particularism-Universalism scale. Specifically, the data presented for the first two control groups, and especially the Croats, suggest that the elements of nationality, locale, and other particularistic concerns will diminish in importance along with further mobilization and development.

21. It should be noted that when controlling for level of socio-economic development, a very similar coefficient (.29) is found for individuals residing in the least developed environments.

22. For purposes of the "culture-region" breakdown, the communes drawn from the Adriatic coast are listed as "Adriatic Coastal" with the republic from which they are drawn following in brackets.

23. Consider, for example, the differences in the distribution of radio and television usage in the most developed (Maribor) and least developed (Nevesinje) communes at the time the survey was taken. Figures showed 36 radios and 16 televisions per 100 inhabitants in Maribor, and only 7 radios and .7 televisions per 100 in Nevesinje. *Statistički Godišnjak SFRJ*, 1969, pp. 519, 523, 571, and 579.

CHAPTER VI

1. The term "elite" will be used to refer to occupations that generally convey positions of high social, cultural, or political status. These occupations will be divided into those positions found in the political realm (to be referred to as "political elites"), and positions in the social and cultural realm (to be referred to as "social elites.") The remainder of the population representing occupations of generally lower status positions will be referred to as "masses."

2. Other research focusing on the elite-mass phenomenon and using the same survey data has shown some rather marked contrasts in belief systems. See, for example, M. George Zaninovich, "Political Elite, Professional Groups and Workers-Peasants: An Analysis of Value Differentiation in Yugoslav Society," in Carl Beck, Frederic J. Fleron, Jr., Milton Lodge, William Welsh, and M. George Zaninovich, *Comparative Communist Political Leadership* (New York: David McKay Co. Inc., 1973), pp. 226-297. Zaninovich has shown that individuals in positions of higher social and political status tend to show the attitudinal characteristics of a "modernizing elite," while those individuals representing the mass sector display lower levels of such characteristics. Perhaps some of these attitudinal contrasts could be traced to different levels of exposure to mobilizing influences.

3. The Workers' Universities, "electrification programs" in rural areas, and improved transit systems are all examples of efforts to close the gaps among different sectors of society.

4. Socialization theory has generally shown that as one's age increases, his propensity for value change decreases. See, for example, the research summarized by Irwin Child, "Socialization," in Lindzey, *Handbook of Social Pyschology*, II, pp. 677-680.

5. The finding suggests that modernizing efforts are not being wasted on the old and that this sector can also change when touched by the stimuli. This finding should be encouraging to Yugoslav planners in view of their vigorous attempts to mobilize older sectors of the society. One important effort has been to develop and expand the Workers' and Peoples' Universities more fully. For an interesting account of the conception, objectives and role of these adult universities, see: Dragomir Filopović, "Workers' Universities, 1959-1968," *Yugoslav Survey*, X (November, 1969), pp. 119-128.

6. This means, for example, that when employing the original scales and correlating mobilization and modernism among the "masses." the majority of respondents fell in low mobilization-modernism categories. As a result, there was not enough dispersion and too many empty cells to yield an accurate measure of the relationship. However, when collapsing the index and two scales, the empty cells were eliminated and an accurate correlation coefficient was produced.

7. Interesting figures are displayed as a result of this general isolation from the change stimuli. Namely, when dichotomizing the traditionalism-modernism scale, only 9 per cent of the masses reflect "modernized" value systems, whereas 40 per cent of the social and cultural elites and 37 per cent of the political elites reflect these value systems. Furthermore, while 13 per cent of the masses rank as universalistic when dichotomizing the particularism-universalism scale, a total of 27 per cent of the social elites and 36 per cent of the political elites assume this more universalistic set of values.

8. It is interesting to note that in his study of individual and political modernization in six countries, Inkeles notes a similar set of influencing phenomena: "Our research indicates that what is lacking in the traditional culture may be provided by the institutions of a modern society—by the school, the factory, the newspaper and the radio. These sources of influence evidently have an independent power to effect political socialization, training men to know more about politics, stimulating them to take an interest in political events and to participate in civic affairs, and fostering a shift in allegiance from tribal and local leaders to those representing a wider community of interest." Inkeles, "Participant Citizenship," p. 1141.

9. Similar contrasts were found between party and non-party sectors in another analysis of the same survey data (although the primary concentration was on a number of different attitudes). For an analysis of these contrasts and the implications they raise for further societal change, see: M. George Zaninovich, "Party and Non-Party Attitudes on Societal Change," in R. Barry Farrell (ed.), *Political Leadership in Eastern Europe and the Soviet Union* (Chicago: Aldine Publishing Co., 1970), pp. 294-334.

10. The same finding applies in the party-member sector as reflected by the .51 coefficient.

11. The change will be greater among the non-member sector for two primary reasons. First, because of their present value sets, they have the "longest way to go;" and secondly, the party member element is more likely to be modernized and universalistic, regardless of their exposure to the mobilization stimuli.

CHAPTER VII

1. For the figures reported herein, see: Sergije Pegan, "Opinions on Relations Between Nations in Yugoslavia." in Firdus Dzinić (ed.), *Yugoslav Public Opinion Concerning Current Political and Social Questions* (Belgrade: Institute of Social Sciences, 1964). Translated by JPRS, 1970.

2. For the full report of these figures, see: Dragomir Pantić, *Ethnic Distance in Yugoslavia* (Belgrade: Institute of Social Sciences, 1967). Translated by JPRS, 1970.

3. The study of "ethnic distance" was based upon the approach of the American sociologist, E. S. Bogardus, who developed the so-called "Bogardus scale of social distance" to explore ethnic and racial attitudes in America.

4. Perhaps the most outspoken critic of the "exploited" position of the developed republics, and in particular Croatia, was Sime Djodan. For his analysis of the nature of the economic problem including the position of Croatia, see: Sime Djodan, "Evolucija Gospodarskog Sustava SFRJ i Ekonomski Polozaj Hrvatske" ("The Evolution of the Economic System of Yugoslavia and the Economic Position of Croatia), *Hrvatski Književni Zbornik*, II (Fall, 1971). Translated and reprinted in *Journal of Croatian Studies*, XIII (1972), pp. 2-102.

5. For an incisive analysis of insecurities, frustrations, and resultant nationalism related to such issues, see: Branko Horvat, "Nationalism and Nationality," *Gledišta*, No. 5-6, 1971. Reprinted in the *International Journal of Politics*, II (Spring, 1972), pp. 19-46.

6. In March of 1967, for example, the Croatian literary and cultural society "Matica Hrvatska" published a manifesto demanding a constitutional change to provide better protection for the literary languages of Yugoslavia and, in particular, the Croatian language. Among other demands, the manifesto requested that the hyphen be taken out of Serbo-Croatian and that they be considered separate languages, i.e., Serbian and Croatian.

7. Stipe Šuvar, "Marginal Notes on the Nationalities Question," *Gledišta*, No. 5-6 (1971), p. 58. This and three other articles by Yugoslav scholars appearing in this issue of *Gledišta* have been translated and are reprinted in the special issue "The Nationalities Question in Yugoslavia," *International Journal of Politics*, II (Spring, 1972).

8. W. G. Runciman, *Relative Deprivation and Social Justice* (Berkeley: University of California Press, 1966), p. 9.

9. One of Yugoslavia's foremost economists, Branko Horvat, has made this statement on a number of occasions. See, for example: Horvat, "Nationalism and Nationality;" also, see his speech at the symposium on "Culture and the New Constitution" as published in the Belgrade literary weekly, *Književne Novine*, May 8, 1971.

10. A great deal has been written on the issue of relative deprivation although it has never been applied, at least to my knowledge, to national sentiments in East Central Europe. For some basic sources on relative deprivation, see: Runciman, *Relative Deprivation*; Ted Robert Gurr, *Why Men Rebel* (Princeton: Princeton University Press, 1970); and Hadley Cantril, *The Pattern of Human Concerns* (New Brunswick: Rutgers University Press, 1965). Cantril's empirical study of aspirations and frustrations in thirteen countries, which does include Yugoslavia, sets out a useful methodology for further studies using the relative deprivation approach.

11. The values most relevant to humans has been a subject of considerable discussion. Although some classifications are more detailed than others, Runciman and Gurr identify three basic sets of values. They are: economic, political, and status. Interestingly, these value sets correspond with the three problem areas identified above. Runciman, *Relative Deprivation*, Ch. 3; and Gurr, *Why Men Rebel*, pp. 25-26. They also correspond with Cantril's empirical findings concerning the three most important aspirations the Yugoslav people had for their nation. Cantril, *The Pattern of Human Concerns*, p. 55.

12. It is worth noting that Šuvar identifies what are generally the same values among the Yugoslav populace although, in my estimation, he seems to confuse or mix them somewhat: "the first is linked to the natural striving of every nation or ethnic community whatever for self-determination and a struggle for an equal place in the contemporary world . . . the second is linked to the economic and cultural perspectives of the societies that are relevant not only for the national and ethnic communities as such but for people . . .and finally, the third is connected with the institutional network of relations among the nationalities." Šuvar, "Marginal Notes on the Nationalities Question," pp. 51-52.

13. Šuvar, "Marginal Notes on the Nationalities Question," p. 50. I have emphasized those values basic to the theory of relative deprivation.

14. It was at this time that mass demonstrations developed in Zagreb. Shortly thereafter, the LCY began its reorganization of the Party leadership in other republics, a move that seemed designed, among other things, to reduce the frustration among the Croats and the sense of an anti-Croat campaign. Subsequent developments suggest that the policy had practical effects.

15. Djodan, "Economic Position of Croatia," p. 77. Djodan's comparison with Norway failed to foresee their joining the EEC "agglomeration."

16. Djodan, "Economic Position of Croatia." p. 95.

17. *Ibid*.

18. This is not to say, however, that the frustrations and national sentiments have been distributed *evenly* across all regions and national groups.

19. Šuvar, "Marginal Notes on the Nationalities Question," pp. 50-51.

20. *Borba*, July 12, 1972.

CHAPTER VIII

1. Deutsch, *Nationalism and Social Communication*, p. 78.

2. Shoup, *Communism and the Yugoslav National Question*, p. 263.

3. Lerner remarks in no uncertain terms: "In every country, the rural villagers declare themselves the most unhappy fellows. In every country, the modernizing individuals are considerably less unhappy—and the more rapidly the society around them is modernized, the happier they are." *Passing of Traditional Society*, pp. 398-399. For some representative expressions of the integration theorists, see: Claude Ake, *A Theory of Political Integration* (Homewood, Ill.: The Dorsey Press, 1967), pp. 3-4, 98-101; and Deutsch, *Nation-Building*, pp. 6-7, 118-119.

4. There may of course be more than two problems encountered during the process of individual change. However, in the author's estimation, the two to be discussed here are the most significant and relevant to the change phenomena being investigated in the study.

5. This does not mean that less sophisticated sectors (e.g., the peasantry) are always susceptible to manipulation and control, as the agricultural collectivization program in Yugoslavia after the war showed. However, it is an accepted fact that poorly trained and equipped populations have less effect upon governments and institutions than more sophisticated sectors. See, for example, the phenomenon discussed in the case of India, in Myron Weiner, *The Politics of Scarcity: Public Pressure and Political Response in India* (Chicago: University of Chicago Press, 1962); and in the case of an extensive number of developing societies, in Gabriel A. Almond and James S. Coleman, *The Politics of Developing Areas* (Princeton: Princeton University Press, 1960).

6. William J. Foltz, "Building the Newest Nations: Short-Run Strategies and Long-Run Problems," in Deutsch, *Nation-Building*, p. 127. For another expression of a similar thesis, see: Mancur Olson, Jr., "Rapid Growth as a Destabilizing Force," *Journal of Economic History*, XVII (December, 1963), pp. 529-552; also see: Bert F. Hoselitz and Myron Weiner, "Economic Development and Political Stability in India," *Dissent*, VIII (Spring, 1961), pp. 172-179.

7. For some works on the self-government idea in Yugoslavia, see: Ante Fiamengo, ed., *Komunisti i Samoupravljanje* ("Communists and Self-Government") (Zagreb: Fakultet Političkih Nauka, 1967); Krsto Š. Kilibarda, *Samoupravljanje i Savez Komunista* ("Self-Government and the League of Communists") (Beograd: Sociološki Institut, 1966); Ichak Adizes, *Participatory Democracy: Yugoslav Style* (New York: Free Press, 1971); and, Sharon Zukin, *Beyond Marx and Tito* (London: Cambridge University Press, 1975).

8. See Daniel Lerner, "Toward a Communication Theory of Modernization," in Pye, (ed.) *Communications and Political Development* (Princeton: Princeton University Press, 1963), pp. 330-333.

9. Samuel Huntington, *Political Order in Changing Societies* (New Haven: Yale University Press, 1968). Also, for another work expressing the same basic theme, see: Samuel P. Huntington, "Political Development and Political Decay," *World Politics*, XVII, 3 (1965), pp. 386-430.

10. One interesting effect of the country-wide televison network is expressed in the following account which was told by a broadcasting official from a station in one of Yugoslavia's six republics. The account noted that one republic suddenly realized that its peasantry was beginning to sing the folk songs of another republic, and that these songs had been picked up through cultural programs broadcast on the country-wide television network. The republic contended that to preserve their own folk tradition, they would have to substitute their own folk programs to override those on the countrywide network and, in fact, did so shortly thereafter.

11. The trend is not only evidenced in value change, but in many other correlates of the change process. That is, an inevitable result of the industrial-technological-cybernetic society seems to be a general movement away from more specific, lower-order cultural activities (e.g., republic, locale, family) to more general, higher-order activities. An interesting study of this type of change in Yugoslavia identified three levels of culture: national, professional, and mass. On the basis of preliminary findings, the study has shown the first level to be declining rapidly in importance while the latter two are growing.

12. For a useful account of the policy trends of the Titoist regime in this regard, see Shoup's chapter entitled, "Titoism and the National Question," *Communism and the Yugoslav National Question*, pp. 184-226.

Date Due

APR 2 1 1987			
NOV 1 2 1990			
DEC 4 1990			